CAESAR'S INVASION OF BRITAIN

NEW YORK UNIVERSITY PRESS · New York

Title page: Roman soldiers fighting
'barbarians' – a detail from the Arch of
Constantine, erected in AD 313–5.

Pages 6–7: The forbidding cliffs of the
South Foreland, the Roman army's first
sight of the island of Britain.

First published in 1978 by Orbis Publishing Limited, London
This edition published in 1980 by New York University Press, New York
Library of Congress Catalog Card Number: 79–90167
ISBN 0–8147–2157–5
Manufactured in Great Britain by Butler & Tanner Ltd, Frome and London

Contents

For Maria V. Soteriades, who shares
an interest in the ancient world.

'*Even Julius Caesar, the first of the Romans, who set his foot in Britain at the head of an army, can only be said by a prosperous battle to have struck the natives with terror, and to have made himself the master of the sea shore. The discoverer, not the conqueror, of the island, he did no more than show it to posterity. Rome could not boast a conquest.*'

—*Publius Cornelius Tacitus*
c. 55–120 AD

'It was clearly no place to attempt a landing'

–CAESAR

It was a fine late summer day in the year of Rome 699. In the early hours of that morning, which later calendars would record as 25 August 55 BC, a fleet of some 80 warships and transports was observed crossing the Straits of Dover towards the British coast. By 9 a.m. the ships were clustered at anchor under the shadow of the great white cliffs of the South Foreland.

Along the cliff-tops, following the shore-line as far as the eye could see, were massed thousands of British warriors, called together by the alarm of their coastal sentinels when the ships had first appeared in the early dawn light. The British chieftains, gathering their warriors into fighting units, looked down on the vessels beneath them with interest and a certain degree of awe, for these ships were packed with seasoned troops of the Roman army–an army which had conquered three-quarters of the known world and which, even now, was fresh from its victories in Gaul, just across the water.

Below, in the prow of one of the war galleys, the 47-year old Roman commander-in-chief, Caius Julius Caesar, returned the Britons' interested scrutiny. He later wrote: 'I saw the enemy forces standing under arms along the heights. At this point of the coast precipitous cliffs tower above the water, making it possible to fire directly onto the beaches. It was clearly no place to attempt a landing.' The general decided to let his invasion fleet ride at anchor while he summoned a meeting of his staff to discuss the situation.

On the cliff-top was gathered an army from the major southern British tribes–the Cantii, the Atrebates and others. The main force

Left: The South Foreland cliffs look directly down to the narrow beach, making a safe landing impossible for an invasion force. The Romans were compelled to sail farther up the coast to find a more suitable spot.

consisted of the Cantii, who were to give their name to their tribal area of Kent, and who were split into four septs under their chieftains Cingetorix, Carnilius, Taximagulus and Segonax. In the hands of these men lay the defence of Britain. These chieftains knew that the alien soldiers on the sea below them had come to force them to submit to the suzerainty of Rome, as their Celtic brethren in Gaul had been forced to submit during the previous year. This much they knew because the Roman commander, who called himself Governor of Gaul, had sent them an emissary: a Gaulish chieftain named Comm.

Comm, whose name the Romans had Latinized to Commius, was the chief of the Gaulish Atrebates, whose territory lay in the region of modern Arras and had been conquered by the Romans in 57 BC. Now, it was claimed, Comm was a friend of Caesar. On arriving in Britain, Comm had claimed overlordship of the British Atrebates, one of the larger southern tribes, whose capital lay near the site of Silchester in Hampshire. Many tribes from Gaul, fleeing from Roman and German expansion, had sought refuge in Britain among their fellow Celts, but other tribes in Britain shared a similar tribal name with the tribes in Gaul. So it was with the Atrebates and also with the Parisi, who gave their name to the modern French capital but who also had a British branch in south-eastern Yorkshire. It was not uncommon for Gaulish or British chiefs to rule tribes in both lands, such tribes being united by a common Celtic language and culture. A generation before Comm, Diviciac of the Suessiones had exercised such power in northern Gaul and in Britain. Indeed, 600 years later Celtic chieftains still ruled simultaneously both in British Cornwall and in Brittany.

Comm, acting as Caesar's ambassador, had told the British chieftains that the Roman terms of surrender were that the British must recognize the supreme authority of Rome, that tribute should be paid to Rome every year, and that a certain number of prominent tribesmen should be handed over as hostages to the Romans to ensure the good behaviour of the tribes. The British chieftains knew that the Roman demands were not to be dismissed lightly. Many people among them were refugees from Roman conquest and oppression.

Among the latest batch of refugees were many of the Veneti, whose tribal area lay along Quiberon Bay in modern-day Brittany and whose tribal capital, Vannes, still bears their name. The Veneti had once had a sea-trading monopoly from the Bay of Biscay, across to Britain and along the coast up into the North Sea. A nation of sailors and fishermen, they had ships capable of facing the heavy seas which rolled in from the

Atlantic. These ships were flat-bottomed, with high bow and stern, and were built solidly of oak, with timbers a foot thick fastened with large iron nails. They had iron chains for cables and their sails were made out of leather in order to bear the strain of the weather. The Veneti had not accepted Roman rule. During the previous year of 56 BC their fleet of some 220 ships had met up with a Roman fleet in Morbihan Bay commanded by Decimus Iunius Brutus, a cousin to the afterwards famous Marcus Brutus. After a battle which lasted from 10 a.m. to late evening, the fleet of the Veneti was destroyed. At the same time, Caesar and his legions had devastated their townships.

The Veneti prisoners were sold into slavery, and those who could escape had made their way to Britain. The refugees' tales of Roman military prowess left the British chieftains with no illusions. The British had decided to send the Roman general a vaguely worded message which appeared to indicate their willingness to submit to Rome. Caesar had then embarked for Britain, under the watchful eyes of British agents.

The Roman invasion force, utilizing the captured ships of the Veneti, consisted of only two legions, the VIIth and the Xth, not more than 10,000 troops. The main bulk of the Roman army was to be left in Gaul under the command of General Quintus Titurius Sabinus and General Lucius Aurunculeio Cotta. The Romans had few men to spare for a campaign in Britain because the conquest of Gaul was by no means an accomplished fact. A number of tribes in Normandy were still in a truculent mood and had not formally submitted to Rome, and there was also a great deal of resistance in Aquitane. A prominent Gaulish chieftain named Dumnorix of the Aedui was secretly trying to raise a more general insurrection against the Romans. At any time the tribes of Gaul could strike against the tenuous 'Pax Romana'.

The unsettled situation in Gaul and the news of the smallness of the Roman invasion force had delighted the British chieftains. The tribal armies of the Cantii, Atrebates and their western neighbours could muster many times the number of Roman troops and throw them back into the sea before they even set foot on the shore. Now, during that fine morning of 25 August 55 BC, the British warriors waited confidently along the cliff-tops of the South Foreland for the Romans to begin their landing.

CHAPTER 1

'The land at the extremities of the earth'

-TACITUS

The majority of the Roman troops crossing the Channel that night of 24/25 August knew nothing of the country to which they were sailing. Indeed, most of them knew only that they were going to 'the land at the extremities of the earth,' as Tacitus later called it. For many of them, the invasion fleet might well be sailing over the edge of the world. But if they had such fears they kept them to themselves and trusted to the leadership of their commander-in-chief. A hundred years later, during the Roman invasion of 43 AD, the Roman soldiers were not so trustful and there was a near-mutiny because, in the words of Dio Cassius, 'the soldiers were indignant at the thought of carrying on a campaign outside the limits of the known world'.

But to what extent was Britain an isolated and unknown country? One of the earliest references to Britain was made by Herodotus (484–407 BC), who spoke of the *Cassiteriades* or Tin Islands lying to the north-west of the known world. While disclaiming any detailed knowledge of the country or its people, he speaks of 'the Tin Islands from which tin comes to us', showing that already Britain had a trading link with the Mediterranean world.

In the fourth century BC, Pytheas, a native of the Greek colony of Massilia (Marseilles), visited Britain and travelled over a considerable part of it. He mentions the fact that the British were agricultural and pastoral farmers whose main crop was wheat: 'This wheat the natives thresh, not on open floors, but in barns because they have so little sunshine and so much rain'. He added that inland the British kept large herds of cattle and sheep. In Cornwall he found that the British were workers of iron, tin

Left: The earliest distinctive form of Celtic writing was the simple Ogham script developed in Ireland. Some 300 memorials with Ogham inscriptions, like this one from Kilmalkedar, Co. Kerry, can be found in Ireland, while 57 survive in Britain.

13

Above and right: Examples of the ingenuity of British Celtic metalworkers, contradicting Caesar's descriptions of the 'backwardness' of the natives. Decorated metalwork was used for many purposes, including personal ornaments and (top right) horses' bits.

and bronze, made fine pottery and were spinners of wool and weavers of cloth.

'A stormy strait separates the shores of Britain which the Dumnonii hold, from the Silurian island,' wrote Pytheas. The Silures were a tribe in South Wales and Pytheas wrongly thought that the Bristol Channel separated Britain from Wales. The Dumnonii still lived in the same tribal lands when the Romans invaded and they gave their name to the modern county of Devon. 'This people,' says Pytheas of the Dumnonii, 'still retain their ancient customs. They refuse to accept coin and insist on barter, preferring to exchange necessities rather than fix prices.' Coinage did not develop in Britain until the second century BC.

Another writer, whom Caesar probably read before his expedition, was Diodorus Siculus, who died c. 21 BC. In his *World History* he cited several older writers as his authorities on Britain, including Timaeus and Posidonius. Siculus gave a very interesting and accurate account of Cornwall: 'The inhabitants of that part of Britain which is called Belerion [Land's End] are very fond of strangers, and from their intercourse with foreign merchants, are civilized in their manner of life. They prepare tin, working very carefully the earth in which it is produced. The ground is rocky, but it contains earthy veins, the produce of which is ground down, smelted and purified. They beat the metal into masses like *astragali* and carry it to a certain island off Britain called Ictis . . .

14

here, then, the merchants buy the tin from the natives and carry it over to Gaul, and after travelling over land for about 30 days, they finally bring their loads on horse to the mouth of the Rhone.' Siculus accurately describes the method of tin streaming, the working of 'earthy veins', which was a means of gathering surface tin. And archaeology in Cornwall has revealed some of the goods – Iberian brooches, Grecian mirrors and other artefacts – which were exchanged by merchants for the tin long before Caesar set foot in the island.

Both Pytheas and Siculus left descriptions of Britain which hardly agree with the picture that Caesar later presented of the inferior British knowing nothing of agriculture or weaving, living only on meat and dressing in skins.

It must be remembered that the writers of Rome and Greece, quite obviously, presented a foreigner's view of the British society and culture and, with some notable exceptions, looked upon the people of Celtic Britain as barbarians and savages. Roman descriptions of Celtic society, such as Caesar's own account, are written from the viewpoint of the superiority of a conqueror bringing civilization to savages – a justification for imperial expansions across the centuries. Naturally enough, the ideas and interpretations of the Romans were very biased and mostly erroneous. After all, one would hardly expect soldiers of Lord Chelmsford's army to give a fair account of Zulu social and military institutions. It is true that Caesar questioned many Celts about their social system, but the information given often shows either a misinterpretation of ideas or the fact that the Celts deliberately gave wrong information to confuse the conqueror. Such misinterpretations can easily occur, for it is often hard for a person of one cultural outlook to grasp another fully unless he has studied it for some time. An eminent English historian once wrote that the kingship in Celtic Scotland was a very bloody business, for hardly ever did a son succeed a father to the throne. From the English standpoint, with the feudal concept of hereditary right, the observation is fair. However, in Celtic culture there was no such thing as primogeniture, and rulers were elected – elected from the family which was familiar with the duties of chieftainship, but elected nevertheless. Therefore the observation becomes absurd and presents a totally distorted view of Celtic history. We must bear in mind that Greek and Latin observers, including Caesar himself, were also open to such misconceptions.

The British at the time of the Roman expeditions were a Celtic people; the earliest Greek references to Britain mention Celtic place-

16

names. The Celts constituted an ancient civilization which left its mark from Asia Minor to Ireland. They were the first Transalpine people to emerge into recorded history. According to the ancient Greek chroniclers, who designated them *Keltoi,* they originated from the region around the Lower Danube. The Celts were a linguistic group and not a racial one. Professor Eoin Mac Neill has pointed out that there is no such thing as a Celtic *race* any more than a Latin race, a Teutonic race, or a Slavic race. The peoples of Europe in this respect are a mixture of several races and, for the most part, the same races, though not in the same proportions. This admixture was true of ancient times, as can be observed by the various descriptions ancient writers gave of the 'typical' Celt: the swarthy, stocky Silurian Celt was equally typical with the tall, gangling, blond Gaulish Celt.

The language which the British tribes spoke was the Brythonic (named after them) branch of the Celtic language. This was the ancestor of Welsh, Breton and Cornish, which have survived and developed into modern times. Gaulish, of which there survives only a few inscriptions, also belongs to this Brythonic family; it may be that the Britons and the Gauls spoke the same language or one that was mutually intelligible.

The other branch of Celtic is Goidelic, from which have descended Irish, Manx and Scottish Gaelic.

The main differences between the two branches of Celtic are that the Brythonic languages have simplified themselves in their case-endings and in the losing of the neuter gender and dual number. The two groups also differ in the matter of initial mutation and aspiration. There is the famous substitution of P for Q in the Brythonic languages which has caused some scholars to label the two branches as P and Q Celtic. This was the sound which in Indo-European, from which Celtic, along with most other European languages, descends, gave *qu (kw)*. This sound *qu* in Goidelic later became represented by the *c*. The *qu* in Brythonic was replaced by *p*. For example, the numeral 'four' in Irish is *ceathair* while in Cornish it is *peswar*. More readily recognized examples can be found in the following:

English	son	head	worm	feather	everyone
Irish (Q)	mac	cenn	cruiv	cluv	cach
Welsh (P)	map	pen	pryv	pluv	paup

Although a form of writing in Greek characters was known among the Celts in Caesar's time and was used for a few inscriptions, Celtic

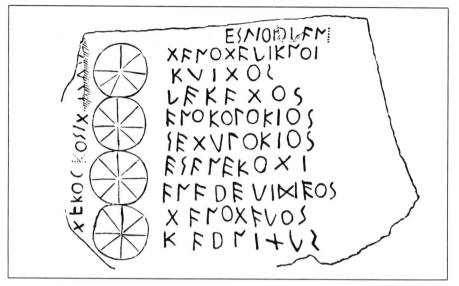

writing did not develop until well after the birth of Christ. This illiteracy in their own language was by design, as Caesar pointed out: 'The Druids think it unlawful to commit this knowledge of theirs to writing (in secular and in public and private business they use Greek characters). This is a practice which they have, I think, adopted for two reasons. They do not wish their system should become commonly known or that their pupils, trusting in written documents, should less carefully cultivate their memory; and, indeed, it does generally happen that those who rely on written documents are less industrious in learning by heart and have a weaker memory.' History, geneaology, folklore and mythology, poetry and the strict laws by which they were governed, were all committed to memory by the druids and bards. In having to learn such things by heart, Caesar comments that it sometimes took as long as 20 years before a druid or bard qualified.

The first form of Celtic writing was developed by the Goidelic Celts of Ireland with a script called Ogham. It has been argued that the Ogham inscriptions were carved in a language which was no longer generally spoken and that it was a 'religious language' used by the druids in the same way as people sometimes use Latin today for sacred reasons on monuments. Irish was the first of the Celtic languages to be written extensively and now contains Europe's oldest vernacular literature.

In Caesar's day, Brythonic Celtic was the common language of

Britain. The Celtic occupation, aside from the areas of Wales, Scotland, and Cornwall, where they have remained until modern times, can clearly be seen in the place-names of England. Geographically descriptive words such as 'crag', 'dun' and 'cumb' or 'combe' abound in modern-day English place-names. The Celtic word for river—*avon*—has caused several English rivers to be so named. Indeed, the majority of English rivers bear Celtic names such as the Alne, Anker, Arrow, Cole, Leam, Penk, Soar and Trent in the Birmingham area alone, not to mention the greater rivers such as the Thames, Severn, Douglas and Ouse. Mountains such as the Pennines and Mendips and forests such as Kesteven, Barroc, Andred, Penge, Lyme, Arden, Cannock, Morfe, Kinver and Savernake still retain their Celtic names. Many modern English towns and cities also bear their original names, including London, which derived from the words 'Lug' or 'Lugh', a Celtic god, and 'dun', meaning a fortress. The same place-name was given to Lyon in France, whose name developed from *Lugdunum,* the Latinization of the Celtic name. One of

Left: Britain had an extensive trade with Europe long before Caesar came. This Italian wine cup was found in a Celtic grave at Welwyn, Hertfordshire. The graveyard contained many examples of Mediterranean imports.

the first British Celtic settlements discovered by the Romans was Dover, or *Dubrae* as they Latinized it from the Celtic, which means 'the place of the waters' and referred to the streams there. The Welsh still have the word *dwfr* for water, while the Cornish word is *dovr* and the Breton is *dour*.

It is generally thought that the first Celtic migrations to Britain took place about 600 BC, but modern scholarship has suggested that the first Celtic-speaking peoples may have arrived as early as 2000 BC—definitely no later than the middle and late Bronze Age (somewhere around 1500 to 1000 BC). The last series of migrations of individual tribes occurred in the second century BC when the Belgic tribes of Gaul arrived in southern Britain to escape from the pressures of Roman and German expansion.

The Celts were not the first people to live in Britain. They found another people occupying it and absorbed them in the same way that the French and English are trying to absorb the remnants of the Celtic civilizations today. A unique feature of the Celtic languages is that, while they are classified as Indo-European and have Indo-European vocabularies, much of their syntax is not Indo-European. The linguist Sir John Morris Jones suggested that the survivals were similar to the idiom of the Hamitic languages, which include Arabic, Hebrew, Ethiopic, Berber and ancient Egyptian. How such survivals from one language to another are possible may be seen from the Irishman who says, in English but with Irish grammar, 'I'm after going down the road' meaning 'I have gone down the road' or the Cornishman who says in correct Cornish word order, 'Going home, are 'ee?' meaning 'Are you going home?'. Languages and cultures can rarely be entirely eradicated.

At one period of their history the Celtic peoples dominated northern Europe. In the fourth century BC they began an expansion into Italy. They captured Rome in 387–6 BC and Polybios tells us that the Romans remained under Celtic domination until 349 BC, when they began successfully to fight back against the invaders. By 345 BC the Celtic conquest had been turned back, but a large proportion of Celtic settlers did remain in northern Italy (Cisalpine Gaul) down to imperial Roman times, leaving evidence of their settlements in such places as Trevi, Treviso, Treviglio, Reno, Milan, Bologna, the River Trebia and other places which have obviously Celtic place-names.

This stay in Italy also resulted in some Celtic words being borrowed from Latin: words such as *gladius* (sword); *scutum* (shield); and *vates* or *ovates* (philosopher or soothsayer). According to the scholar Henri Hubert the Latin writers of the time benefited from the imagination of the Celtic poets: 'The story of the Gallic Wars, out of which Livy, a historian of genius gifted with the spirit of divination, has made a very remarkable historical work, is something quite by itself, rather fabulous and very epic. Monsieur Jullian (Camille Jullian, *Histoire de la Gaule,* Paris, 1920) has suggested that the tradition was probably made up of Celtic epics. The well-known story of Valerius Corvus, who was rescued in single combat with a Gallic chief by a crow which pecked the Celt's face and hid the Roman from him with its wings, is an example. The episode is unlike anything else in Roman history or literature. But it is like a famous episode in the great Irish epic of Ulster, the *Tain Bó Cuailgne,* in which the goddess Morrigu attacks Cuchulain, who has scorned her love, in the form of a crow. The crow is not a mere flight of fancy; it is the creature which stands for battle and the gods and goddesses of war.' It might also be added of Valerius Corvus that Corvus is Latin for crow.

The Celts continued to be a threat to Rome for many years, and it is perhaps ironic that the first time the Germanic peoples (ancestors of the English and Franks) emerge into recorded history, they are seen fighting for the Celts–'undoubtedly as hired troops or as forces levied on a subject territory', says Professor Eoin Mac Neill. Scholars such as Mac Neill and Carl Marstrander have pointed out that a number of words of Celtic origin are found in the whole group of German languages: 'Some of these words are especially connected with the political side of civilisation and are therefore especially indicative of Celtic political predominance at the time of their adoption into Germanic speech'. The Germans first emerge into recorded history in the Roman *Acta Triumphalia* for the year 222 BC when it is told how the Romans, led by the consul Marcellus, won the battle of Clastidium (Casteggio, northern Italy) and defeated the Celts led by Virdumarus.

At the same time as their expansion towards Rome, the Celts began to push into the Balkan Peninsula and during the next century they entered Greece. The Macedonians were unable to impede their progress and the Celtic armies divided into three sections and started to advance into the Greek interior in 260 BC. The eastern army, commanded by Cerethrois, attacked on the Bulgarian side, while the western army, commanded by Bolgios, entered Macedonia, defeated the Macedonian army and slew their king, Ptolemy Cereaunos. The central army, commanded by Bran or Brennus and Achichorius, advanced successfully against Haemos and then against Thessaly. The Greek armies were scattered. Bran came to Thermopylae, where an Athenian army was gathered. He routed it and

Above: Celts pillage the Greek sanctuary at Delphi as part of their eastward expansion. This scene of Bran's sack of Delphi was found in an Etruscan grave.

turned on Aetolia and Callion, but his main force came through the gorges of Parnassos to Delphi where they sacked the great temple of the oracle. Although the Greeks finally turned back this Celtic invasion, Thrace remained a Celtic kingdom until 193 BC.

The contacts between the Celts and Greeks resulted in some Celtic words being adopted into Greek, such as *leiousmata* or *leloumata* (a kind of body armour); *ernbrektou* (a kind of soup or porridge); *os* (the kermes oak); *taskos* (a stake); and *karous* (a trumpet).

A large body of Celtic tribes broke away from the invasion force and moved further eastwards into Asia Minor, where they established a state called Galatia. Henri Hubert comments: 'What we know of the Galatian state gives us our first example of the organisation of a Celtic state'. Writing of the 'Commonwealth of the Galatians', the ancient chroniclers were surprised by the intrinsic democratic character of the state: government was by an assembly of 300 elected representatives. Galatia remained a Celtic-speaking country until the fifth century AD.

By the first century BC the Celtic 'empire' had declined and the Celts had been confined to Gaul and the offshore islands of Britain and Ireland. The last attempted territorial expansion had been made in the late second century when a tribe called the Cimbri (shades of the Welsh *Cymru*?) swooped into Italy and destroyed several Roman armies. This led to a drastic reorganization of the Roman army by Caius Marius, who created the ruthless, legionary fighting machine which is so well known today. By 101 BC Marius was making punitive expeditions into Transalpine Gaul, and 40 years later Caesar was completing the subjugation of the continental Celts.

The Celts of Britain must have been watching Caesar's campaigns in Gaul with the certainty that, should he succeed, it would not be long before they would suffer Roman invasions. This, they considered, was a good enough reason for sending warriors and supplies to aid their Gaulish kinsmen and for making Britain a safe haven for refugees from imperial Rome.

CHAPTER 2

'This people still retain their ancient customs'

–PYTHEAS

The ordinary Roman troopers must surely have wondered what manner of people they were facing as their transports approached the gathered tribesmen atop the great white cliffs in that early morning light. Caesar and his staff officers were obviously better informed and knew they were facing a people who were similar in language, manners and customs to the Gauls. Did the Romans find the Britons, as Diodorus Siculus found the Gauls, 'physically . . . terrifying in appearance with deep sounding and very harsh voices'? From what we know of latter-day Celts, Siculus made some interesting generalizations when he wrote of them: 'In conversation they use few words and speak in riddles, for the most part hinting at things and leaving a great deal to be understood. They frequently exaggerate with the aim of extolling themselves and diminishing the status of others. They are boasters and threateners and given to quick bombastic self-dramatization, and yet they are quick of mind and with good natural ability for learning.'

What sort of society did the British Celts have at the time of the Roman invasions? Early Celtic society displayed a primitive communism, or community-ism, which, in the fifth century AD codification of the Brehon Laws of Ireland, became a very sophisticated social system. We can assume that that social system, or its close approximation, prevailed in Britain during Caesar's time because it was a system which was general to all Celtic societies. This may be demonstrated by a comparison of the Irish Brehon Laws with the Laws of Hywel Dda of Wales and the Breton laws embodied in the Treaty of 1532 which brought Brittany under French suzerainty. Even the laws of the semi-

Left: A softstone head showing a typical Celtic stylization of human features. The moustache and eyebrows have become decorative spirals; a characteristic torc decoration is worn around the neck. The head was discovered in Bohemia.

25

mythical ruler of Cornwall, Dunwallo Molmutius, display an intense regard for democracy and the rights of the individual. Dunwallo was said by Geoffrey of Monmouth to have been the son of Cloten, who ruled Cornwall in about 450 BC and 'who established among the Britons the so-called Molmutine Laws which are still famous today'. It has been suggested that when King Alfred (871–909 AD) compiled his famous Anglo-Saxon laws, Asser, the abbot of Amesbury and bishop of Sherborne, a Welsh monk from St David's, translated the Molmutine Laws for the English king, who incorporated some of them.

In essence, the Celtic system was thus: when a tribe occupied a territory it belonged to the tribe as a community. The territory was delimited by natural boundaries and it was then divided for the benefit of the community. Sections of the land were appropriated by the ruler and his civil-service class in return for the work of their position in the society. A large section of land was retained for the use of the entire tribe as common land which everyone, no matter what his station, was entitled to use. This was good pastoral and agriculture land and not unusable land which no one else wanted. Another section of land was set aside for the maintenance of the poor, the old, and incapable members of the tribe. Those who had their own plot were expected to pay taxes for the upkeep of the community, paying for the support of the poor, aged and orphans. If a man fell behind with his taxes and died, the surviving relatives were not made to pay his debts–the Celtic laws humanely stated 'every dead man kills his liabilities'.

The land worked by the chieftains and the erroneously described 'nobles' of Celtic society was not theirs to do with as they willed. There was no such thing as absolute ownership of land, and individual ownership of land was totally foreign to Celtic thought. Each tribesman was able to keep and work his tribal land but he could not sell it, alienate it or conceal it, or give it to pay for any crime, contract or debt. Even the disposal of chattels, such as cattle, had restrictions, and if a tribesman wanted to dispose of any goods he had to seek permission from the tribe.

The extent of common ownership in Celtic society is vividly illustrated by the Irish Senchus Mor's 'Bee Judgement', which stated that the owner of bees was obliged by law to distribute a portion of honey among his neighbours every third year 'because the bees had gathered the honey off the neighbours' lands'.

One of the fundamental institutions of Celtic society was the observance of common rules in agriculture and the existence of a co-operative of several interested parties in agricultural development. Celtic

26

agricultural development was widely praised by Pliny the Elder when he surveyed it in the first century BC. The Celtic plough, he observed, fitted with a mobile coulter, was greatly superior to the Roman swing plough of the same period. The Celts had also developed the art of manuring as well as the invention of a harvesting machine. According to Pliny, 'A big box, the edges armed with teeth and supported by two wheels, moved through the cornfield pushed by an ox; the ears of corn were uprooted by the teeth and fell into the box'.

The principles of common ownership survived for a surprisingly long time. In Scotland, for example, W. F. Skene observed: 'Yet though the conscious Socialist movement be but a century old, the labouring folk all down the ages have clung to communist practices and customs, partly the inheritance and instinct from the group and clan life of their forefathers and partly because these customs were their only barrier to poverty and because without them social life was impossible.' As late as 1847, says Skene, there were still places in the Outer Hebrides where the land was tilled, sowed and reaped in common and the produce divided among the workers in accordance with the old Celtic ways. The old feast of *Nábachd* (*Nábaicheadh*—neighbourliness) was still held, when men drew their plots of land by lot. The produce of certain plots was set apart for the poor and fines went to a common fund to buy fresh stock. John Rae, writing in the *Fortnightly Review* in 1895, says the communal system was still current in Islay and St Kilda, where they 'distributed the fishing rocks among themselves by lot', while in Barra 'they cast lots once a year for the several fishing grounds in the deep seas off their shore'.

Celtic society appears to have had six basic social classes, but it was possible for a person to rise from the lowest order of society to the highest and likewise fall in the same manner. Position in society was granted according to ability and service to the community. There were few cases of people achieving military distinction who were rewarded by grants of land from the community; unlike feudal society, military service was not a criterion for status.

Starting with the lowest social grading there were the 'non-freemen'; it is impossible to use a more explicit term. Certainly these were not slaves; the idea of one man holding another in servile bondage was completely alien to Celtic philosophy and the later codified Celtic laws were uniformly averse to slavery. These non-freemen were law-breakers. A law-breaker suffered a loss of civil rights, cessation of pensions, and prohibition from practising the professions or being employed in the civil service. There were no prisons—the law-breakers suffered a loss of civil rights within the community, temporary or permanent, unless they could satisfy the fines imposed on them. Celtic society was against taking away the physical freedom of the offender, preferring simply to prevent him or her from being elected to any position of trust in the society until he had redeemed himself. Offenders were not altogether excluded from society but were placed in a position where they were forced to make a contribution to its welfare. The non-freemen consisted not only of criminals but also of cowards who deserted the tribe in time of need, prisoners-of-war, and hostages. Prisoners-of-war and hostages could be returned to their tribes on payment of a tribute. A third-generation non-freeman was automatically granted a full citizen's rights. Although no non-freeman was allowed to leave the tribal territory without special permission, he had freedom to acquire, by service, his own plots of land.

The next social grading was the tribesman who did not work his own plot of land but merely hired himself out as a herdsman or worker on others' lands. He took part in the military muster of the tribe as a full citizen but, because he was classed as 'itinerant', he had little political say.

The basis of Celtic society was the tribesman who worked his land, paid taxes for the upkeep of the community, formed the army in time of war, and worked out political decisions and ideas by means of an electoral system, electing local assemblies to administer the tribe's affairs.

Above the tribesman was what the Romans erroneously described as the nobility. The error comes from trying to equate the Celtic system with terms in a totally alien system. These 'nobles' were, in fact, a 'civil service' class, public officers elected by the people to carry out the administrative work of the local assemblies. The 'civil servant' was assigned land for his use while he was alive in return for his duties. These duties were to receive taxes; to act as executive officers for the welfare of the community; to keep roads and bridges in repair; to supervise the running of the tribal hospital, the orphanage, the poor homes, and the public hostels; to maintain the public mill and the public fishing nets; to exercise police duties; to arrange entertainment for visiting dignitaries; and in time of war to organize the army and act as quartermaster-general. He also had to make sure the farmers of the tribe were well supplied. If a tribesman had a surplus of stock he had to inform the 'civil servant' so that if another was short a balance could be kept.

Then came the professional classes: the druids, the bards, the lawyers and doctors. The druids have been, again erroneously, called a 'religious caste' who fulfilled not only religious functions but political ones as well. They were certainly not a caste, and anyone in the tribe could undertake the strenuous training required to become a druid. This is not to deny that there were some druidic families, in much the same way as some families carry on certain professions today. The function of the druid was basically as minister of the Celtic religion, which had a complete doctrine of immortality and a moral system and which was spread among all the Celtic peoples. The druids were also philosophers, teachers and natural scientists who were often called upon to give political and military advice.

Caesar described them in these words: 'They are concerned with religious matters, perform sacrifices offered by the State and by private individuals, and interpret omens. Many of the youth resort to them for education and they are held in high honour by the Gauls. They have the decision in nearly all the disputes that arise between the State and individuals; if any crime has been committed, if any person has been killed, if there is any dispute about an inheritance or a boundary, it is the druids who give judgement; it is they who settle the rewards and punishments. Any private person or any tribe refusing to abide by their decision is excluded from the sacrifice. This is the heaviest punishment that can be inflicted; for those so excluded are reckoned to belong to the godless and wicked. All persons leave their company, avoid their presence and speech, lest they should be involved in some of the ill consequences of their situation. They can get no redress for injury and they are ineligible to any post of honour.'

As Caesar correctly observed, the druids were trained in 'international' law as well as tribal law and were arbiters in disputes between territorial groups. The druids had the power to prevent warfare between two Celtic tribes, for whatever their differences the moral and legal authority of the druid was greater than the tribal ruler's. Siculus comments: 'And it is not only in the needs of peace but also in war that they [the Celts] carefully obey these men and their song-loving poets, and this is true not only of their friends but also of their enemies. For oftimes as armies approach each other in line of battle with their swords drawn and their spears raised for the charge, these men come forth between them and stop the conflict as though they had spellbound some kind of wild animals. Thus, even among the most savage barbarians anger yields to wisdom and Ares does homage to the Muses.'

Caesar seemed surprised that 'the druids do not serve in military campaigns and do not pay taxes along with their fellow countrymen.

They are exempted from all civil duties as well as from military service. These privileges,' he adds cynically, 'induce a great many to submit themselves voluntarily to druidic training while many others are sent by their parents and kinsfolk. These pupils are said to learn by heart a vast number of verses. Some, in consequence, remain under teaching for as many as twenty years'. As we have seen, at this time all the religious teachings, laws, history and folklore of the various Celtic tribes were committed to memory and told to the people as an oral tradition. This was not because the Celts could not write, but because they wanted these things to remain secret.

The Celtic religion was one of the first to evolve a doctrine of immortality. The druids taught that death is only a changing of place and that life goes on with all its forms and goods in another world, a world of the dead which gives up living souls. Therefore a constant exchange of souls takes places between the two worlds; death in this world brings a soul to the other and death in the other world brings a soul to this world. Caesar wrote: 'The druids' chief doctrine is that the soul of man does not perish but passes after death from one person to other. They hold that this is the best of all incitements to courage as banishing the fear of death. They have much to say about the stars and their motions, about the magnitude of the heavens and earth, about the constitution of nature, about the power and authority of the immortal gods. And this they communicate to their pupils.'

Caesar's somewhat cynical remark that this religious outlook could have accounted for the reckless bravery of the Celts in battle was echoed by Pomponius Mela (c. 43 AD), who wrote: 'One of their dogmas has come to common knowledge, namely, that souls are eternal and that there is another life in the infernal regions, and this has been permitted manifestly because it makes the multitude readier for war. And it is for this reason too that they burn or bury with their dead, things appropriate to them in life, and that in times past they even used to defer the completion of business and the payment of debts until their arrival in another world. Indeed, there were some of them who flung themselves willingly on the funeral pyres of their relatives in order to share the new life with them.'

As for the other philosophies of the druids, Aristotle, Sotion and Clement all state that early Greek philosophers borrowed much of their philosophy from the Celts. The similarity of druidic philosophy, especially on immortality, and Pythagorean philosophy has frequently been stated. Pythagoras had a slave named Zalmoxis of Thrace, who

Right: The oldest extensive document in a Celtic language – the famous calendar found at Coligny, near Bourg, France, dating from the first century AD. Latin characters and numerals are used, but the language is Gaulish. Each month is marked by the abbreviations 'MAT' for a good month and 'ANN' for a bad month.

30

appears to have been a Celt. But while Clement of Alexandria says that Pythagoras and the Greeks acquired philosophy from the Celts, presumably through Zalmoxis, Hippolytus claims that Zalmoxis took Pythagoras' philosophy to the druids: 'He, after the death of Pythagoras, having made his way there, became the founder of this philosophy for them'.

Cicero pays tribute to the druids as great natural scientists who had a knowledge of physics and astronomy applied in the construction of calendars. The earliest known Celtic calendar, dated from the first century AD, is far more elaborate than the rudimentary Julian one and has a highly sophisticated five-year synchronization of lunation with the solar year. This is the Calendar of Coligny, now in the Palais des Arts, Lyons, in France. It consists of a huge bronze plate which is engraved with a calendar of 62 consecutive lunar months. The language is Gaulish but the lettering and numerals are Latin. Place-names, personal names and inscriptions on the calendar testify to a certain degree of literacy in the Celtic language. In Celtic fashion, the calendar reckons by nights. Caesar explained: 'They count periods of time not by the number of days but by the number of nights; and in reckoning birthdays and the new moon and new year their unit of reckoning is the night followed by the day'.

The Calendar of Coligny is a masterpiece of calendrical calculation and proves Caesar's statement. The knowledge of calendars and astronomy intrigues many scholars today, who speculate whether the Celts could have arrived in Britain as early as 2000 BC—for recent surveys have shown Stonehenge to be a large astronomical computer, and it may be that the druids were, after all, responsible for such constructions.

The Celtic year was, in fact, divided into four major religious festivals. The feast of *Samhain,* starting on the evening of the last day of October and continuing on 1 November, marked the end of one pastoral year and the beginning of the next. It was a time when the Celtic Otherworld became visible to mankind and when spiritual forces were let loose on the human world. The festival was taken over by Christianity and renamed All Saints' Day or All Hallows' Day. The evening before became Hallowe'en, which is still celebrated as the night when evil marches across the world, when spirits and ghosts set out to wreak their vengeance on the living.

The next great festival occurred on 1 February, which was the feast day of a Celtic goddess known as Brigit in Ireland and as Brigantia in Britain. Her cult was widespread throughout the Celtic world. The feast

32

was connected with the coming into milk of the ewes and was therefore a pastoral festival. Christianity, unable to supress this tradition, turned Brigit into Saint Brigid so that the people could still celebrate her feast day without reverting to 'pagan superstition'.

The third festival was the feast of *Beltane* on 1 May. The Irish word for the May month is still *Bealtaine* and, until the nineteenth century, Scottish law continued to name its May term as the Beltane term. The name derives from the Celtic words meaning the Fires of Bel. Bel was one of the major gods of the Celtic world, representing the sun, the life-force of the world. Inscriptions and place-names concerning Bel are to be found across the Celtic world as far as northern Italy. In Scotland, May Day was known as *Lá Buidhe Bealltuinn,* the golden-yellow day of the Fires of Bel. It was an apt description, for the whins would be in bloom across the hillside making a golden-yellow arc and the tiny whinchat, the small bird which frequents the yellow gorse, would add its colouring to the vivid yellow.

Beltane was the day when the Celts offered praise to Bel, the sun, for having brought victory over the powers of darkness and for bringing the people within sight of another harvest. On that day the fires of every household would be extinguished. Then, at a given time, torches would be kindled by the druids from the 'sacred fires of Bel' (i.e. from the rays of the sun) and taken to each house, where the fire would be rekindled to give each household a fresh start in the eyes of Bel. Also, a number of cattle from each herd were driven in the ancient circles through fires as a symbol of purification. Scholars are, in fact, at variance as to whether Beltane was the start of the Celtic New Year, in view of the symbolism of starting life afresh. The consensus of opinion, however, is that Samhain started the year.

It is interesting to note that, in Cornwall, the Old Cornwall Societies have preserved the folk tradition (which lasted until World War I) of lighting May Day bonfires, a ceremony whose origin is now half-forgotten among the Cornish. There is a ceremony held in the Cornish language during the ritual lighting of the flames.

The last ceremony of the year was the feast of *Lughnasa* on 1 August. It was named after the Celtic god whose creative role often confuses him with Bel and who was known as Lugh in Ireland, Lud in Britain, Lugus in Gaul and Lleu in Welsh mythology. He gave his name to several places, notably London and Lyon in France. The feast of Lughnasa was basically an agrarian feast in honour of the harvesting of crops, and the celebration usually lasted for 15 days. August is still called *Lúnasa* in Irish,

34

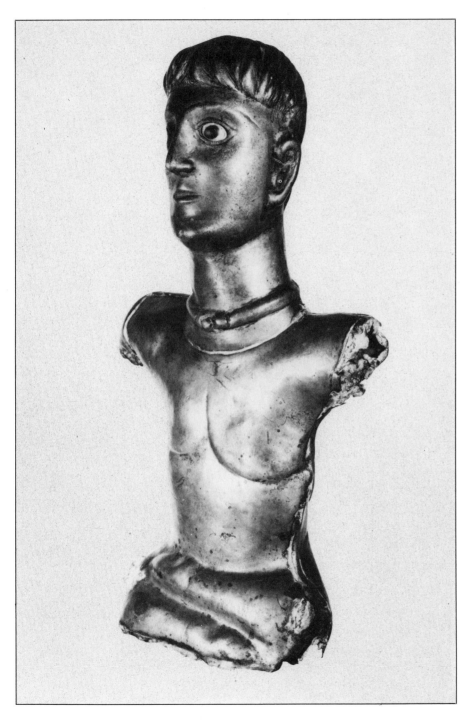

Left: Supposedly the Celtic god Cernunnos, this bronze figure was found at Bouray, France, and dates from the third century BC. It wears a torc around its neck and sits in the traditional yoga position. Celtic customs, and particularly laws, show many close parallels to Hindu customs.

whereas the Brythonic Celts have adopted the Roman name.

Caesar regarded Britain as the headquarters of the druids. 'The system of the druids is supposed to have been invented in Britain and to have been introduced from that country into Gaul. To this day those who are anxious to make themselves more completely acquainted with it frequently visit the island for the purpose of study'.

In this regard Caesar was not accurate. The druids were native to all the Celtic peoples and their theological and social philosophies were universal in the Celtic system. It is true, however, that when Gaul fell to Rome, first Britain and then Ireland became the bastion of druidism, which eventually succumbed to Christianity.

The 'internationalism' of the druids was a cornerstone for the solidarity of the Celtic world. Henri Hubert has pointed out that Celtic societies from as far as Asia Minor to Ireland were in communication and inter-connected. The Senate of Marseilles, during the Roman campaigns in Asia in 197–6 BC, used the influence of the Gauls to persuade the Galatian Celts not to supply Antiochus III and to recruit mercenaries on behalf of the city of Lampsacos. According to Hubert: 'This solidarity of the Celtic peoples, even when distant from one another, is sufficiently explained by the sense of kinship, of common origin, acting in a fairly restricted world, all the parts of which were in communication. But the Celts had at least one institution which could effectively bind them together, namely the druids, a priestly class expressly entrusted with the preservation of traditions. The druids were not an institution of the small Celtic peoples, of the tribes, of the *civitates;* they were a kind of international institution within the Celtic world, with provinces corresponding to the great racial or territorial groups constituted by Ireland, Britain and Gaul. Caesar tells us that the druids of Gaul were in touch with those of Britain, and Irish tradition gives evidence of the relations of the druids of Britain and Ireland. It is certain that this priesthood, provided . . . with a legal doctrine, a moral doctrine, a doctrine of the immortality of the soul, and an authority recognized by all, covered the greater part of the Celtic world, and it is almost unthinkable that it did not cover it all. The bonds which united the Celtic peoples were made secure by the spread of druidism, and we can be sure that those peoples owed to those professional teachers moral ideas, conceptions about the future life, mythological traditions, ritual practices, and legal solutions which they all had in common – that is, that similar principles everywhere governed or reformed the structure and working of society.'

36

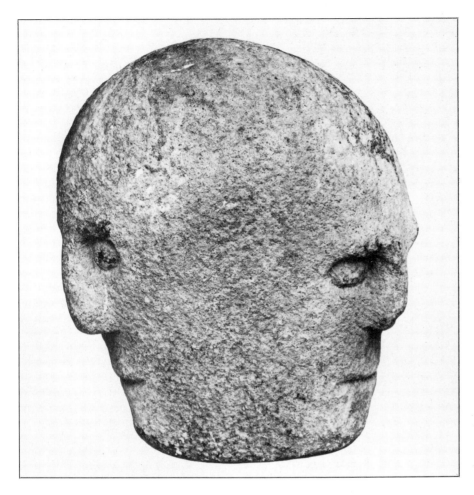

Left: Another typical Celtic head stylization is seen in these two faces from a tricephalic stone head found in Corleck, Co. Cavan, Ireland.

Closely associated with the druids was a professional class of minstrels and storytellers. Diodorus Siculus observed: 'They have also lyric poets whom they call Bards. They sing to the accompaniment of instruments resembling lyres, sometimes a eulogy and sometimes a satire.' Later Celtic writings showed that the bards were a highly trained, professional group who were the repositories of Celtic folklore, legends, history and poetry. They held a salaried position in the retinue of a chief.

Training a bard was probably as lengthy as training a druid because, as we have already seen, the tradition was an oral one. The Celtic bards had to learn by heart the traditional stories, poems and folklore, and they had to be word-perfect. This oral literature can hardly be comprehended by

us today, although the tradition survived in remote parts of Ireland and Scotland where crofters would gather around an aged *seanchaí* and listen to him recite his stories. Woe betide him if he put a word out of place, because his audience would often as not know the tale word-perfectly themselves.

Already, in Caesar's time, the Celtic bards would have to commit to memory heroic tales which constituted a rich and colourful mythology. Most Celtic myth is heroic, for the Celts made their heroes into gods and their gods into heroes. In the lives of these heroes, the lives of the people and the essence of their religious tradition is mirrored. Celtic heroes and heroines were no mere physical beauties with empty heads. The Celtic hero and heroine had to have intellectual attributes equal to their physical capabilities.

As a people, the Celts had a strong natural feeling for learning and

Above: The Celts were fond of music and had a wide variety of instruments. At top is the terminal disc from this trumpet found at Loughnashade, Ireland.

intellectual exercise. Greek and Roman writers have often remarked on this aspect of their temperament, contrasting it with what they considered to be the crudity of their material civilization but praising the refinement and elegance of their use of language and appreciation of linguistic subtlety. In modern times, many visitors to the Celtic countries have recounted stories of meeting an Irish crofter or a Welsh postman, a Scottish labourer or Breton farmer, who has discoursed with them on philosophy and literature in such terms as would put a university man to shame.

The Celtic bards were also quick-witted; Posidonius, quoted by Athenaeus, described how quick a poet had to be with his compositions by citing an incident during a feast in Gaul given by a chieftain named Louernius: 'A Celtic poet who arrived too late met Louernius and composed a song magnifying his greatness and lamenting his own late arrival. Louernius was very pleased and asked for a bag of gold and threw it to the poet who ran beside his chariot. The poet picked it up and sang another song saying that the very tracks made by his chariot on the earth gave gold and largesse to mankind.'

In poetry, song and musical accomplishment, the Celts delighted. Posidonius, Athenaeus and Diodorus Siculus noted the popularity of music among the Celts and made mention of a variety of instruments including lyres, drums, and pipes. A harp-like instrument was also played, and archaeologists have discovered a form of trumpet. A seventh-century BC decorated pot from Sopron, Hungary, of Celtic origin, has an illustration of a lyre. Celtic mythology is full of stories of musicians which show that music was one of the basic passions of the Celts. Greek and Roman writers confirm this, adding that both instrumental and vocal music was widely popular at Celtic social gatherings. We find that contests among musicians and poets were a tradition reaching into very ancient times. Likewise, dancing was popular, and dancing figures can be observed on Celtic pottery dating back to the seventh century BC.

The vividness of Celtic music, untarnished by the centuries of foreign domination and influence, can still be heard in the music of the Irish traditional music group, The Chieftains. This group drew its inspiration from the work of the Irish composer Seán Ó Riada, who died at the tragically early age of 40 in 1971. Ó Riada was trained in the European classical tradition and, after studying serial music in Paris, he returned to Ireland to research into Irish traditional music. Forming a group of musicians known as the Ceoltóirí Chualann, Ó Riada produced several records before his death. His music caught the heart and soul of Celtic music, a music raw and sweet at the same time. Moreover, it is a music uninfluenced by medieval Latin church music, which has dominated most other European folk cultures. Irish music still retains its pentatonic scale basis, sharing it only with African and Chinese music. The revival of the real Irish traditional music has today become almost a world cult. The Greek composer, Christos Pittas, in an interview in the Irish magazine *Hibernia,* 4 February 1972, said: 'What Ó Riada achieved is the revelation of a living cultural tradition which, to most Europeans, was undiscovered and unknown. Some philosophers have tended to judge societies and countries by their musical traditions, and that Ireland has such a music, with such personality and depth, is indicative of a great culture.'

Ending our survey of the six basic Celtic social classes, we come to the chieftain, the last and highest social grading in Celtic society. There was a whole scale of chieftains ranging from the tribal chief to the provincial chief and to an overall ruler or 'High King'. It would seem that the concept of a High King ruling many tribes who united in paying him allegiance was in effect in Caesar's day in Britain, and the ready allegiance given by the southern tribes to Caswallon of the Cassi in 54 BC is indicative that he held such an office.

All chiefs were elected. They had to be capable of carrying out the responsibilities involved, and were therefore usually elected from one particular family used to the problems that a chief encountered – but, it must be stressed, there was no such concept as primogeniture. It was difficult for a chief to usurp power, for he was limited and hemmed in by the democratic process of the tribal assemblies and he was so dependent on his tribe for support that it was easier for him to promote their welfare and safer for him to conform to the intention of the law than become either negligent or despotic in office. Therefore, when Caesar writes that the southern British chiefs excused themselves for imprisoning his ambassador by saying that they had been forced to do so by 'the common people', it could well have been the truth of the matter. Although to Roman eyes it was ridiculous for a chief to be dictated to, in Celtic society the tribal assembly could well give its chief such orders.

Celtic chieftains, in strong contrast to Roman leaders, were not in any sense law-makers but simply officers of the established law. A chief was president of the tribal assembly, commander of the forces in war and usually a judge in the public courts. On the whole, he was more like the president of a democratic republic.

40

One of the things found remarkable by the Romans was the fact that women could rule as chiefs of Celtic tribes on their own merits. The status of women in Celtic society and their social prominence have been found remarkable by many scholars. The female had a unique place in Celtic society compared with other civilizations. She could be, and was, elected as chief. She could lead her tribe as military commander, as the Icenian Boudicca, or Boadicea as the Romans called her, did just over a hundred years after Caesar's invasion. In Celtic mythology there is ample evidence of women taking an unrestricted part in public life, such as Medb of Connacht, who was a skilful military chief of staff, as was Grace O'Malley of Connacht in Queen Elizabeth I's day.

Celtic women enjoyed an equality of rights which would have been envied by their Roman sisters. The Roman bride fell *in manu mariti,* through coemption, and belonged to her husband's family; she could no longer own her property. The Celtic woman remained mistress of all she brought into a marital partnership. The husband had no rights over any property she had. Any personal dowry, such as presents received from relatives, also remained her property, which, in the event of the dissolution of the marriage by divorce or death, she took back along with her own freedom and any acquisitions she had made during her marriage, or a proportion of them regulated by law. Any land property managed by the wife remained hers under the jurisdiction of the tribal assembly and the Celtic laws on the commonality of property. Offences against the honour of a woman caused the imposition of heavy penalties in Celtic law.

Caesar was shocked when he wrote: 'Ten or twelve men have their wives in common; brother very commonly with brothers and parents with children. The offspring of each wife is reckoned to belong to the husband who first married her.' Caesar could not grasp the essential commonality of Celtic society, in which the entire tribe lived as a close-knit unit, sharing all responsibilities including the raising of all its children. Therefore, parents with work to do were free to follow that work and able to leave their children safely in the care of the tribe. A very strict and detailed code of laws on fosterage existed and continued to exist under the Brehon Laws. It is also true that a sophisticated form of polygamy existed in which man and woman had equal rights. In Scotland, many centuries later, an interesting form of tracing ancestry was evolved in which descent was traced through the female–for, it was argued, one can never be sure who the father was but one is always sure of the mother.

CHAPTER 3

'The Cantii are the most civilized'

–CAESAR

'Of all the Britons,' wrote Julius Caesar, 'those that inhabit the lands of the Cantii [Kent] are the most civilized and it is a wholly maritime region. These Cantii differ but little from the Gauls in habits of life. But many of the inland Britons do not grow corn. They live on milk and flesh and are clothed in skins. All the Britons stain their persons with a dye that produces a blue colour. This gives them a more terrible aspect in battle. They wear their hair long, shaving all the body except the head and upper lip.'

In this erroneous description, Caesar is even at odds with other Greek and Roman writers–writers like Pytheas, who, three centuries before Caesar, described a more advanced British civilization. Caesar, of course, did not advance into the interior of Britain, and therefore his inaccurate description could have two possible explanations. Firstly, it could be that he was airing the jaundiced view of the Roman 'master-race' or, secondly, the astute Britons could have fed him this wrong information in order to persuade the Romans that Britain was simply not worth conquering.

Caesar's description of the southern British wearing their hair long and shaving their beards, leaving long moustaches, was fairly accurate and, as he remarks, they differed little from their cousins in Gaul. Diodorus Siculus also mentions that the Celtic men shaved their cheeks and grew long moustaches which covered their mouths. The Celts were very fastidious over their personal appearance and soap (*sopa*) was, according to Diodorus Siculus, a Celtic invention. They also used various cosmetic solutions and many of them dyed their hair. Before a battle

Left: A Roman silver coin showing the head of a Gaul, thought to be the Celtic chieftain Vercingetorix. It demonstrates how the Celts shaved their cheeks and stiffened their hair before going into battle.

43

Above: A Celt with a long moustache and with hair brushed straight back from his forehead. This miniature bronze head was found at Welwyn in Hertfordshire.

they were known to wash their hair in lime to stiffen it and then brush it back from the forehead like a horse's mane; thus we find the Greeks and Latins talking about the long, stiff hair of the Celts. The predilection for make-up was apparently well known in the Roman world, for the poet Propertius once reproached his mistress for making-up like a Celt!

The Celts, according to the Greeks and Romans, wore a form of clothing which made them immediately distinguishable as a national entity, in much the same way as a kilt denotes a Scotsman today. This is also confirmed by native sources. Many of the men wore trousers, which were strange to the toga-wearing Romans. In fact, the Romans later adopted tight-fitting trousers for their cavalry and, ironically, it was from the Celts that the Greek geographer Strabo (63 BC–21 AD) says 'the best of Roman cavalry is recruited'. When the Romans established a permanent garrison in Britain, the Celtic trousers (*bracae*) were adopted as part of their uniform, and they must have been much more comfortable in the colder northern climate. These trousers reached to the knees, and sometimes women were known to wear them as well. Usually, however, women would wear a tight-waisted, bell-shaped skirt which had elaborate decorations or was hung with little bells or balls. Decorated pots from the seventh century AD show women clad in such skirts and engaged in spinning and weaving.

Over these garments were worn tunics, usually of linen, which would reach either to the knees or just below the waist. They were caught in at the waist with a girdle, often decorated in bronze and gold. Over this a cloak was worn by women and men alike and fastened by a brooch of gold or silver. It was made of wool, light in summer and heavy in winter. Dio Cassius, describing Boudicca, says: 'She wore a great twisted golden necklace, and a tunic of many colours over which was a thick cloak, fastened by a brooch'.

These woollen cloaks (*sagi*) became famous in the Roman world, just as Scottish tweed or tartan is famous today. Mainly produced in Britain, they were subject to a heavy Roman tax and their excellence and fame were indicative of the skill and prosperity of the sheep-rearing and woollen industries of Celtic Britain. Strabo, in mentioning that Britain exported these woollen cloaks to Italy, again destroys Caesar's erroneous idea that the British did not know anything about weaving!

The common dress of the British in Caesar's day, therefore, would have been trousers for the man, a short linen tunic and a long woollen cloak. Leather shoes and sandals were also worn and sometimes linen shoes with soles made of leather. Sandals of wood were also known to

44

Left: This Roman bronze of a Gaulish prisoner shows the characteristic tunic, trousers and cloak worn by the Celtic male.

have been in use. Headwear hardly ever seems to have been worn, except for a few elaborately worked metal helmets for warriors in time of battle. As previously observed, the Celts were fond of elaborate hairstyling which made headwear superfluous.

Strabo, in describing Belgic Celtic clothing, says: 'They wear the *sagus,* let their hair grow long and wear baggy trousers. Instead of ordinary tunics they wear divided tunics with sleeves, reaching down as far as the private parts and the buttocks. Their wool is rough and thin at the ends, and from it they weave the thick *sagi* which they call *laenae.*' An interesting observation is that the word for shirt in modern Irish and Scottish Gaelic is still *léine.*

Diodorus Siculus sums up: 'They wear a striking kind of clothing—tunics dyed and stained in various colours, and trousers, which they call by the name of *bracae;* and they wear striped cloaks, fastened with buckles, thick in winter and light in summer, picked out with a variegated small check pattern . . . some wear gold-plated or silver-plated belts round their tunics.'

From Diodorus Siculus's remarks we can see that the famous tartan was already in being. And, as he shows, the Celts were fond of personal adornment with jewellery. Strabo disapprovingly comments: 'To the frankness and high spiritedness of their temperament must be added the traits of childish boastfulness and love of decoration. They wear ornaments of gold, torques on their necks, and bracelets on their arms and wrists, while people of high rank wear dyed garments, besprinkled with gold. It is this vanity which makes them unbearable in victory and so completely downcast in defeat.'

While we cannot suppose these descriptions were indicative of all Celts at one given peiod, we can see from such descriptions the intense love of decoration and of wearing individualistic and distinctive clothing. And we can see from the foregoing that the Celts of Britain would be dressed in similar style to their Gaulish cousins and not, as Caesar says, clad only in skins. The Britons were among the foremost spinners, weavers and dyers of woollen garments.

Throughout Britain the people lived mainly in agricultural tribal communities, sometimes centered around a hill-fortress. They were a stable and industrious population, tilling the soil and keeping livestock. Caesar himself noticed the large herds of cattle and flocks of sheep, and Celtic mythology confirms that wealth was measured in cattle. In the epic the *Tain Bó Cuailnge,* three-quarters of Ireland go to war with Ulster over the possession of a great bull. This is the Irish equivalent of the

Right: A Celtic head with the traditional decorative torc, dating from the fourth century BC. This was found at Rinkeby, Denmark.

46

Right: Examples of Celtic
decorative metalwork in gold
and silver. Torcs were worn
around the neck in the manner
of a collar. They appear to
have a socio-religious
significance as all images of
deities and all Celtic heroes
appear to wear them. We are
told in the sixth-century Welsh
poem 'Y Gododdin' that the
300 warriors who went to their
death at Catterick were all
'gold-torced'.

48

49

Above and right: One of the most spectacular pieces of Celtic art from the first century BC is this cauldron found at Gundestrup in Denmark. Its workmanship is in silver and gilt, while the basis consists of an iron bowl which holds the five internal and (originally) eight outer plates, on which intricate designs have been made. Scenes such as the bull (above) may represent deities or scenes from history or mythology.

'Helen of Troy' saga, but in Celtic values Helen is replaced by a beautiful bull! The great cattle herds of Ireland were finally destroyed, with the Irish clan system, in the seventeenth century, while in Scotland the Scottish clans still conducted cattle raids into the eighteenth century. In Caesar's time the people of Britain were not only agricultural and pastoral farmers but were advanced in making implements for their work; they were also miners, smiths and potters of considerable ability.

At the time of Caesar's invasion Celtic art in Britain was of a high standard. It was, in retrospect, reaching a climax, because it would soon be submerged after the Roman invasions by a form known as Romano-British art. Celtic society had developed an interesting and complex visual art. Anne Ross says of it. 'It is in this highly original and complex

series of decorative motifs that the Celts make a real and distinctive contribution to the foundations of European culture.' Celtic art was basically a decorative art, inseparable from Celtic religious outlook and mythology. According to Anne Ross: 'Celtic art is miraculous in its utter intensity and amazing variety. It is possible to study a pattern for hours on end and still come no nearer to understanding its intricacies. Rarely are two areas of any design completely identical, and yet, somehow, there is nothing inharmonious in the whole. In asymmetric patterns one is given the impression of symmetry when it is, in fact, virtually impossible to find two identifiable pieces of repeated pattern in many of the examples. The designs are fluid, sweeping and without a clear beginning or end. They simply exist. In their art style, then, we come

*Above: Representations of
Celtic faces are rarely
naturalistic. In this decoration
for the handle lugs of a
bucket, the eyes and the horned
helmet have been reduced to
simple curving shapes.*

very close to the essence of the Celtic temperament. It reflects the
tortuous and subtle nature of their thought-processes, the complexities
of their language; it makes manifest the complicated shifting, oblique
nature of their religious attitudes. In short, Celtic art is an impressive
summing up of all that is fundamental and distinctive in the spiritual life
of the Celts.'

The basic difference between Celtic art and the art of Greece or Rome
was, as Paul Jacobsthal pointed out in *Early Celtic Art* (1944), a matter of
symbolism versus realism. 'To the Greeks a spiral is a spiral and a face is a
face and it is always clear where the one ends and the other begins,
whereas the Celts see the face in the spirals or tendrils; ambiguity is a
characteristic of Celtic art.'

Early Celtic art developed among the Continental Celts and is
classified as the La Tène culture. By Caesar's day it was a spent force. As
an identifiable 'school of art' it had become noticed around the fifth
century BC and was experimental and immature, although it was already

52

producing items showing a distinct and individual expression. Around 325–250 BC archaeologists observe a new Celtic school which they designate the Waldagesheim style, where symmetry became subservient to a more free-flowing pattern of design. Then came a Plastic style, which was contemporary with a Sword style. These styles were generally robust but with less free flow of pattern and much more discipline. By 100 BC the pressure on the Gaulish Celts from Rome and the Germanic tribes had forced the vigour of Celtic art to decline.

Around 300 BC artists in Britain were producing work which differed little from the Gaulish Celtic styles and it seemed that these styles were introduced into the country by the migration of Celtic tribes from Gaul to the north of Britain, among them the Parisi, who settled in Yorkshire. Through the years this style became very much modified and a distinctive British style evolved. During this period (100 BC to 43 AD) southern British artists were producing magnificent bronze mirrors showing some of the finest and most intricate examples of their artistry and a superb precision of workmanship. Like the Celtic illuminated manuscripts of later years, it is almost impossible to compare this art-form with any other. One such mirror, found at Birdlip, Gloucester-shire, has enamel inlays on the handle, and the Mayer Mirror, recovered from the Thames, is considered to be one of the most beautiful examples of these works of art.

Below: Typical of Celtic decorative art was the spiral pattern. This motif is clearly seen on the decorative stone at the entrance to a Celtic burial mound in Co. Meath, which dates back to the Bronze Age.

Right: The famous bronze mirror from Birdlip, Gloucestershire. With its riot of curvilinear patterns, this is one of the finest examples of British Celtic design.
Far right: Another example of bronze decorative work is this scabbard found in Co. Antrim and cast in the shape of a stylized serpent's head.

Iron and bronze were widely used throughout Britain in the production of many decorated articles. Asymmetric patterns were always prominent, although two British 'schools' have been observed, one favouring the linear style and the other a spiral style. Unfortunately no Celtic workshop has ever been found, and there is little knowledge of the tools which the Celtic artist used. It is known that they must have used compasses as well as free-hand design. Some of the finest examples of British Celtic artistry are to be found on the bronze sword scabbards such as one found in Bugthorpe, Yorkshire, which is generally regarded as one of the loveliest pieces of Celtic workmanship. Shield bosses and shields, such as the famous Battersea shield, dating from Caesar's time, gilded and having red glass insets, give fascinating examples of the capability of these craftsmen.

Again disproving Caesar's statement that the interior Britons were uncivilized, it has been ascertained that there was a flourishing school of northern British Celtic art, reaching its height during the years immediately before and after the birth of Christ, and centred in the Dumfriesshire area of Scotland around a flourishing and vital Celtic community. Indeed, from north Britain, and dated the third century BC, comes a beautifully worked pony cap which was probably used for ceremonial purposes because, with other such war-like accoutrements, it is thought by archaeologists to have been too frail for serious use.

One aspect of craftsmanship we know that the British excelled in was enamelling. Many objects were decorated with enamels, including harnesses for the horses. The Romans tended to use a single colour, red, when enamelling. The British, however, greatly perfected the art and made all sorts of variations, sometimes combining blue glass with the enamel to good effect. The Celts had used coloured glass in their workmanship for many centuries. As the British developed this art and began to enamel larger surfaces, they introduced a technique of filling the enamel voids in the metalwork, thereby emphasizing the pattern in the colour of the enamel and that of the metal. Unfortunately, the art of enamelling in the distinctive Celtic style was lost after the Roman conquest, although it survived and continued in northern Britain until the Romans finally swamped the native culture.

Pottery also flourished in Britain, and two distinct types of wheel-made pottery have been observed dating from this period. The pottery was usually made with a black or grey glaze, which seems to have been a favourite colouring for the British potters.

Some of the most fascinating and exciting art objects from this period

55

are the great carved stones, some displaying merely decorative work and others being naturalistic figure sculptures. Such figures have been found throughout the Celtic settlement areas. Anne Ross comments: 'The present corpus of surviving examples leads us to suppose the former existence of a much richer repertoire in this medium than has been suspected hitherto. The religious zeal of the Middle Ages has no doubt accounted for many of them. Others must await discovery either in the ground or in churches or in private collections, where their real nature has not been appreciated, or in the basements of museums.'

Celtic coinage also became a medium for artistic and mythological expression. Caesar says of the British financial system: 'They use copper or copper coins or bars of iron carefully made to a certain weight, as money.' In fact coinage was introduced to Britain by the Belgic Celts in the second century BC and these coins were spread as far as the Humber and the Severn. The coinage was issued by individual tribes and many of these British coins were of gold and silver.

Most of the Celtic coins had a head on one side and a pattern based on an animal on the other. The heads are presumed to be Celtic gods while the animals range from horses to boars, lions, bears, cattle, goats and

Near right: A Celtic head of the first century AD found at Gloucester. Far right: a stylized horse's head in metalwork from the first century AD. This was found in Yorkshire in some Brigantian fortifications.

Above: 'The Long Man of Wilmington' in East Sussex—an intriguing piece of Celtic art, carved in the chalk of the hillside.

eagles. Chariots also appear on some of the coins. The earliest Celtic coins were struck by the Celts of Transylvania in silver and showed mythological symbols. As the Celts came under Roman influence, their coinage became inscribed with the tribal name.

Caesar also mentions the iron bars of standard weight which were used as currency. Some of these have been found and appear to be unfinished swords used by tribesmen of the west as a means of barter.

'Tin is found in the inland parts,' says Caesar, 'iron near the coast, but the quantity of this is but small.' This 'iron near the coast' is most probably a reference to the iron-fields of Sussex which were worked down to the end of the seventeenth century. Of the other metals to be found, and which were being worked by the Britons at the time, Caesar is silent. No mention is made of the highly sophisticated bronze smelting which must have been widespread throughout the country.

Of building materials Caesar was again in error when he recorded: 'They have timber of all kinds found in Gaul except fir and beech'. And in marching through southern Britain, Caesar observes: 'The population is numerous beyond all counting, and very numerous also the houses. These closely resemble the houses of Gaul.'

57

We can now be sure that when Caesar marched through Kent, he was not seeing crude mud and wattle huts. The British were living in tenemented half-timbered buildings which rose up as high as three storeys.

Modern scholarship is rapidly changing its ideas of Celtic civilization, for, if the monoliths found in Ireland, Britain and Brittany are attributable to the Celts and not to a pre-Celtic people, then the Celts were no mean builders. It has already been discovered that they built fairly good roads, but instead of building them of stones, as did the Romans, they built them with wooden materials which were not generally preserved for archaeologists to find. Celtic roads only came to notice when a part of such a road was found in Europe recently in a boggy area, where it had become fossilized. That roads existed in Celtic Europe should have been obvious from the writings of Diodorus Siculus. Strabo does, in fact, mention roads in Narbonnensis.

That there were roads in Britain at this time may be confirmed by the extensive use of chariots by the British tribes and the ease with which Caswallon conducted his chariot campaign. It is known that transportation among the Celts was by chariot, wagon, horseback and pack horse. While marvelling at the extraordinary system of Roman roads, it may be argued that many of these roads were merely the utilization of previous roads which the Romans improved and systematized. According to Anne Ross: 'Archaeological evidence can as yet determine little of the nature of Celtic roads before the development of the superbly engineered and systematized network of Roman roads throughout Europe. But, just as Roman temples and eventually Christian shrines tended to be constructed over the foundations of pagan sanctuaries, so one may suppose the Romans to have built some, at least, of their sophisticated roads over the ancient tracks which had been proved by their predecessors to have been the most efficient and practical cross-country routes for trading and transport in general. Traces of actual roads do remain and can be determined, when, for example, they run through cemeteries. Coffin tracks have always been vital and known and marked by such things as barrows or, even at the present day, mounds of stones, at which the coffins containing the remains of the dead were rested.'

Causeways were certainly constructed across bogs and marshes with layers of trees, brushwood, earth and stones trampled down to form a firm base and then overlaid with trees or planks. Celtic bridges were constructed of wood. When their laws were codified, the Celts made

specific regulations about maintaining the efficiency of the roads and bridges. Cormac, in his ninth-century AD glossary, echoing the older Brehon Laws, says: 'A road of whatever class must be cleaned on at least three occasions, that is, the time of horse-racing, winter and war'.

With the so-called 'revelation at Clickhimin', in Scotland, it has been found by archaeologists that the Celts also built substantial stone fortresses. These 'brochs', made of dry-stone walling, survive to heights over 40 feet and have the general appearance of the base of a lighthouse. The stone walls had only one small lintelled entrance and inward tapering walls (sometimes 15 feet thick) with chambers, galleries and stairs. These stone fortresses, which were once spread over Britain, have been dated from the fourth and second centuries BC. With this type of building in mind, puzzling references in Irish and Welsh mythology now become clear. Archaeologist Patrick Crampton has stated: 'The evidence of Clickhimin is so revolutionary that it will take years before its full implications can be realized.'

The British countryside therefore flourished with communities living within fortresses and stone buildings of several storeys, a civilization not, perhaps, as advanced in building techniques as Greece or Rome, but certainly not as backward as Caesar would have us believe.

The Celtic fortress of Maiden Castle in Dorset is an example of how

Above: Ruins of a Celtic 'broch' at Clickhimin dating back to the fourth century BC. The existence of such structures debunks the idea that the Britons in Caesar's day only lived in crude mud huts.

59

intricate and extensive Celtic defence systems were at this period. Maiden Castle, from the Celtic *Mai dun* – Mai's fort – stands near Dorchester, once the capital of the Durotiges. Vespasian and his II Augustus Legion were to reduce it during the Roman conquest of 43 AD. It was a stupendous fortress whose earthwork ramparts, rising to a height of 100 feet, enclosed two-thirds of a mile in length and a third of a mile in breadth, dominating the countryside.

In addition to roadways, Celtic Britain was also connected by ferries which plied their trade on the rivers and straits. These were subject to strict regulations in early Celtic law. Strabo mentions ferries as being particularly established among the Celtic tribes, and in Welsh mythology we find that when the Irish ruler Matholwch wishes to cut off communication with Britain he is advised to 'set a ban on the ships and the ferry-boats and coracles'.

The Celts were famed for their skill as boatmen and Strabo commented that they 'have a natural ability for seafaring'. Caesar's famous battle with the Veneti was to prove this, and Strabo wrote an interesting account of Veneti ship-builders: 'After the tribes already described the rest belong to the Belgae, who live along the ocean. Among these are the Veneti, who fought the naval battle against Caesar. For they used the trading station there, and were ready to hinder his voyage to Britain. He defeated them easily by sea, not using rams for the timber of their boats was thick, but when they bore down upon him with the wind the Romans tore down their sails with long-handled hooks; for their sails were made of leather, owing to the force of the winds, and chains pulled them up instead of ropes. They make their boats with broad bottoms and high sterns and prows, on account of the ebb tides. The material is oak, of which they have a large supply, and therefore they do not joint their planks closely, but leave openings which they stop with seaweed, so that when the boats are in dock the wood may not dry up for lack of moisture, the seaweed being naturally rather moist, while the oak is dry and without fat.'

In the early centuries of the Christian era the Celtic Picts of northern Britain possessed a navy which acquired a fearsome reputation. F. T. Wainwright, in *The Problems of the Picts* (1955), writes: 'They possessed a fleet of considerable strength, which implies navigational skill, familiarity with difficult waters, and a knowledge of ship building'.

How was British Celtic society governed? We have already examined the social system and the attitude of Celts towards private property, a concept which was alien to them. Celtic law was a very complex system

60

which finds its closest parallel in traditional Hindu law. D. A. Binchey, investigating 'The Linguistic and Historic Value of the Irish Law Tracts' (1943), found that 'Irish law preserves in a semi-fossilized condition many primitive Indo-European institutions of which only faint traces survive in other legal systems derived from the same source.' Although the Welsh law system (the Laws of Hywel Dda) was influenced by Roman legal concepts and terms, comparisons can be easily made. What is fascinating is that until the fifth century AD the Celtic legal code was transmitted orally in accordance with the universal Celtic custom. Probably it was transmitted in the form of verses to facilitate their learning. The task would seem pretty formidable, especially when we consider how complicated the law system must have been.

Basically, dispute could lead only to arbitration and compensation. The death penalty for a crime was only enacted in extreme cases and never applied to women. Women who murdered were usually sent into exile. It was for the injured party to compel the injurer to accept the arbitration and under the law there was a custom of ritual fasting – the 'hunger strike' – as a method of asserting one's rights. Ritual fasting is, of

Above: Part of the earthwork ramparts of Maiden Castle in Dorset, giving an indication of the extent of Celtic fortresses. Maiden Castle was finally reduced by Vespasian and the II Augusta Legion during the invasion of 43 AD.

61

course, an integral part of Hindu philosophy. If the injurer ignored the fast and wouldn't accept a fine imposed by the judges, he lost his honour, a terrible situation in Celtic society where honour was highly cherished.

One of the most progressive aspects of Celtic society was its attitude to medicine. The Germanic tribes simply used to put their sick and feeble to death. Even in the civilizations of Egypt, Assyria, Babylonia and Greece, there was no provision made for the ailing poor. And the Romans regarded disease as a curse inflicted by supernatural powers and rather sought to propitiate the malevolent deity than to organize relief work. There were notable exceptions to the general rule–men like Hippocrates of Greece–but it was not until about 400 AD that Fabiola is said to have founded the first hospital in Rome under Christian auspices.

About 300 BC Ard Macha (Armagh in Ulster) boasted the foundation of a hospital by the semi-mythical ruler Macha. Although the story belongs to Irish mythology, it is true that the Celts, at a very early stage of their civilization, developed a medical service, a Europe-renowned surgery system and a prototype 'national health service' whereby sick maintenance (including curative treatment, attendance and nourishing food) had to be made available to all who needed it. Under Celtic law the responsibility of providing for the sick, wounded and mentally handicapped was in the hands of the tribe. The exceptional working of this system was undoubtedly due to the tribal organization. Celtic tribesmen did not have to fear illness; they were assured of treatment, hospitalization and the fact that the society would not let them or their dependents lack food or means of livelihood.

The qualifications of physicians were also carefully supervised under law and 'quack' doctors were liable to severe penalties. The Celts recognized that it was rather easy to deceive people who were ill and who, desperately seeking a cure, would grasp at any straw to secure it. Large fines were imposed on quacks who pretended to be qualified surgeons. The law was similarly strict about the condition in which the tribal hospital should be kept.

The ability of Celtic surgeons has been endorsed by archaeologists who have found skulls on which trephining operations have been carried out. In 1935 at Ovingdean, Brighton, a human skull was found dating to about 100 BC. Two large round holes had been deliberately cut in the skull, one on either side of the brain. There had been a healing of the bone showing that Celtic surgeons had performed brain surgery, cutting away the bone of the skull, and, not only that, but the patient had survived the operation; and not merely one operation, but two! Similar skulls have been found throughout the Celtic world, showing that such operations were almost a standard medical practice.

In addition to the laws which governed the running of the tribal hospital there were laws which also governed the running of tribal hostels. Travellers were afforded the utmost hospitality, and each tribe had its public hostel which was looked after by a full-time public hostel manager. He maintained the roads leading to the hostel and kept a light burning all night in accordance with the law to aid travellers.

We can see from this that British society in Caesar's day was anything but primitive and, in reality, was a highly complex civilization with many progressive elements to it. But even at this stage Celtic society was showing a social weakness: the Celts were displaying an addiction to strong and heady liquor. Diodorus Siculus, along with many other writers, commented on the vast quantity drunk by the Celts at their feasts. This often led to quarrels among them, and such events are even confirmed by the native tradition in Irish mythology: such a quarrel is illustrated in the tale of *Bricriu's Feast*. Even Celtic women were known to become drunk and quarrelsome.

The common drink amongst the Celts was an intoxicating ale called *cuirm,* referred to in Gaulish as *corma*. Basically it was made of barley, although rye, oats and wheat could also be used as a base. The grain was converted into malt (*brac* or *braich*) and then dried in a kiln until it was hard. The ground malt was made into a mash with water and this was fermented, boiled and strained until the process was complete. Most families made their own ale, although there were also professional brewers.

Posidonius, writing in the first century BC, and quoted verbatim by Athenaeus in 200 AD, claims: 'They also use cumin in their drinks'. He adds: 'The drink of the wealthy class is wine imported from Italy or the territory of Marseilles. This is unadulterated, but sometimes a little water is added. The lower classes drink wheaten beer prepared with honey'. Mead, based on honey, was perhaps the most characteristic of the Celtic drinks at this time.

The drink most associated with modern Celts, whiskey or whisky, depending on its Irish or Scottish origin, did not come into being until the twelfth century. Whiskey takes its name from an anglicization of the Gaelic *uisce beatha* (Irish) or *uisge beatha* (Scots), meaning 'the water of life'. But its fermentation was dependent on the use of a still, which was not invented until the twelfth century. The first actual reference to whiskey was made in the Irish Annals about 1405 AD.

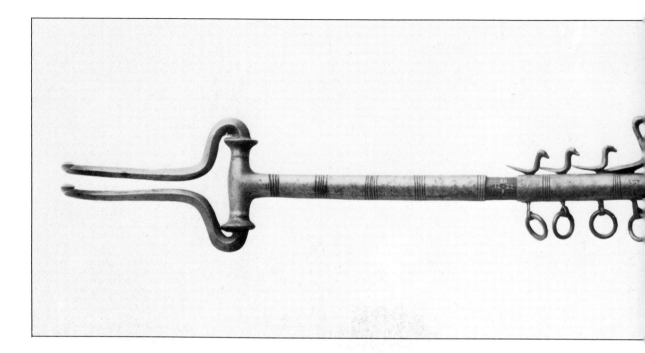

Above: A fleshfork from Dunaverney, Ireland, decorated with ravens and swans. According to Irish myth ('The Story of Mac Da Thó's Pig') at a banquet 'There were seven cauldrons, with an ox and a salted pig in each of them. And the person who came that way would thrust the fleshfork into the cauldron, and whatever he obtained with his first thrust, he ate, and if he obtained nothing at the first attempt, then he did not get a second'.

The Greek and Latin writers were fascinated by the Celtic feasts. Posidonius, describing a feast given by the Gaulish chieftain Louernius, said: 'He made a square enclosure one and a half miles each way, within which he filled vats with expensive liquor and prepared so great a quantity of food that for many days all who wished could enter and enjoy the feast prepared, being served without a break by the attendants.' In Irish mythology, when Bricriu prepared his feast for Conchobar Mac Nessa, he was reported to have gathered food for a whole year and built a special house at Dun Rudraige in which to serve it. We can be sure that such feasts were the order of the day among the British Celts as well.

One of the interesting points about Celtic feasts was the disposal of the Hero's Portion. Athenaeus says: 'And in former times, when the hindquarters were served up, the bravest hero took the thigh piece, and if another man claimed it they stood up and fought in single combat to the death'. Diodorus Siculus confirms this by saying: 'Beside them are hearths blazing with fire, with cauldrons and spits containing large pieces of meat. Brave warriors they honour with the finest portions of the meat.' The Gaulish Celts never seemed lacking in a variety of food. Of the food eaten by the Britons, Caesar remarks: 'They hold it unlawful to

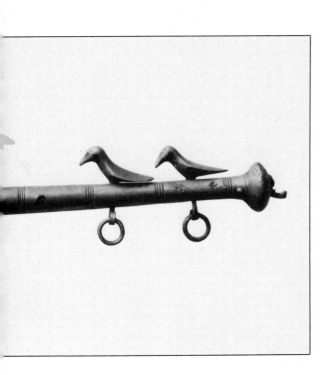

Above and left: Bronze wine flagons of the fourth century BC from the Moselle area. The one above right demonstrates intricate craftsmanship. The little duck on the spout is evidently unaware that it is menaced by the two animals on the lid and the larger animal which forms the handle.

eat hare, chicken or goose. Still, they rear these animals for the sake of amusement.'

We can assume, however, that in dietary habits the British Celts were not so different from their Gaulish cousins. Athenaeus, again quoting Posidonius, records: 'Their food consists of a small number of loaves of bread together with large amounts of meat, either boiled or roasted on charcoal or on spits'. He adds that in coastal areas or near rivers the Celts 'eat fish in addition, baked fish, that is with the addition of salt, vinegar and cumin'. Certainly fish was highly thought of as a food, and one favourite Celtic dish was baked salmon with honey and herbs. In the *Tain Bó Cuailgne,* mention is made of edible seaweeds such as carrageen—seaweed is still used in cooking in Ireland and Scotland today, while in Wales seaweed is also used in dishes like laver bread. Dairy produce was prominent in the Celtic diet, but beef and pork were the mainstays of the meals. 'They have large quantities of food,' wrote Strabo, 'together with milk and all kinds of meat, especially fresh and salt pork'. With the use of salt and other herbs the Celts were able to preserve meat killed in the autumn and store it for winter use.

In spite of the Celts' seeming excesses in drinking and eating, the Greek and Roman writers noted that they were very conscious of their figures, and this is supported by early Celtic writings. Strabo goes on to say: 'They try not to become stout and fat-bellied, and any young man who exceeds the standard length of a girdle is fined'. Whether, in fact, the Celts went so far as to impose a tax on the overfed cannot be confirmed, but it was certainly true that a pot-belly was regarded with scorn.

Apart from feasting, the British Celts found many ways of relaxing and enjoyed games which ranged from the intellectual to the purely physical. Games played a very important part in Celtic life at this time. The Celts seem to have evolved their own form of chess, which, while not chess as we know it, consisted of two sets of men pegged into positions on a wooden board. This game is often mentioned in Celtic mythology. In Ireland the game was called *fidchell,* 'wooden wisdom', and that it was common to all Celts may be seen from the same game in Welsh mythology being named *gwddbwyll,* meaning exactly the same thing.

In the story of *The Wooing of Étain,* the god Midir plays the game for days in a row with Eochaid Airem, the King of Ireland, and the stakes are Eochaid's beautiful wife Étain. In this Irish myth the board is referred to as being made of silver and the pieces of gold. The same type of silver and

allowed to
swiftness. It
too, was po

In many
society of
behaviour v
society no
Theoretical
the basis for
local and ce
the Celtic s
weakness w
such as Ron
the way to

One wea
The Celts
rule–policy
countless ei

gold board is referred to in a Welsh myth when the game is again played for high stakes in *The Dream of Rhonabwy*.

There was another Celtic board game, which was known as *brandub* or 'the black raven'. Celtic gaming pieces and dice from Caesar's day were found recently in a Belgic Celtic grave at Welwyn Garden City.

While such intellectual exercises and games were doubtless very popular among the Celts, they also enjoyed physical sports. One of the earliest recorded field games was hurley, a game rather like hockey. The game is mentioned in early Celtic mythology and its existence is confirmed by illustrations on Celtic pottery. A clay mould found at Kettering has a figure carrying a hurley stick and ball. A plaque found at Hockwold-cum-Wilton, Norfolk, also shows a man with a hurley stick in his right hand and a ball in his left. In the *Tain Bó Cuailgne* we are told that the Irish hero Cu Chulainn excelled in hurley, and there is an interesting passage about the hero as a boy at play:

'The boy went forth and took his playthings. He took his hurley stick of bronze and his silver ball; he took his little javelin for casting and his toy spear with its end sharpened by fire; and he began to shorten the journey by playing with them. He would strike his ball with the stick and drive it a long way from him. Then with a second stroke he would throw his stick so that he might drive it a distance no less than the first. He would throw his javelin and would cast his spear, and would make a playful rush after them. Then he would catch his hurley stick and his ball and his javelin; and before the end of his spear had reached the ground he would catch its tip aloft in the air'.

As well as playing field games the Celts loved hunting, and they indulged in it as much out of pleasure as necessity. Strabo mentioned the special significance given by the Celts to bird hunting. He records that 'there is also a wooden weapon resembling the *grosphus* which is thrown by hand and not by means of a strap, with a range greater than that of an arrow and which they use mostly for bird hunting as well as in battle'. Bird hunts, which also had a religious significance, are quite prominent in Celtic mythology.

Among the southern British tribes, which Caesar encountered, hunting with dogs was very popular, and, especially among the Cassi, breeding hunting dogs was considered an art. One of the most popular forms of hunting was for wild boar or pig, which were venerated as Otherworld or magical animals, although this did not prevent the Celts from hunting and eating them. Hunting boars is another popular theme in Celtic mythology. Strabo says of the Belgic Celts: 'Their pigs are

67

an unfordable river, he would either swim or propel himself across it on an inflated skin; and often arrived at his destination before the messengers whom he had sent ahead to announce his approach.'

As a military commander, Caesar was enormously popular with his troops. He always addressed his men as 'comrades' and 'he judged his men by their fighting record, not by their morals or social position, treating them all with equal severity – and equal indulgence; since it was only in the presence of the enemy that he insisted on strict discipline. He never gave forewarning of a march or a battle, but kept his troops always on the alert for sudden orders to go wherever he directed. Often he made them turn out when there was no need at all, especially in wet weather or on a public holiday. Sometimes he would say "Keep a close eye on me!" and then steal away from the camp at any hour of the day or night expecting them to follow. It was certain to be a particularly long march and hard on stragglers.' Nevertheless, the troops loved their eccentric general, for when he felt they deserved relaxation he let them run as wild as they pleased. In answer to one of his critics he said, 'My men fight just as well when they are stinking of perfume.'

But he was also keen on regimental pride, and his legions were always smartly turned out on parade. He always believed in telling his troops the truth of their position before a battle, even when the advantage was against them. He did not believe in feeding his men false courage. No legion ever mutinied under his command and when the Civil War started his men did not hesitate to serve him without pay.

It was as a general that he was admired by Rome and later generations of soldiers. His tactics were adopted by the German generals of World War II in their conception of the 'blitzkrieg' or 'lightning war', for Caesar's greatest successes were due to the rapidity of his movements, which brought him on the enemy before they heard of his approach. He travelled sometimes 100 miles a day, reading or writing in his carriage. Sometimes the strength of his own character would steady his troops when they were on the verge of panic. He once seized a panic-stricken standard-bearer, turned him round and told him that he had mistaken the direction of the enemy. But he was not a reckless commander. He never exposed his men to unnecessary danger and his losses in the Gaulish campaigns were exceptionally slight.

Cicero said of Caesar that as an orator he surpassed every other contemporary. As a writer Cicero's praise of him is more gracefully emphatic. Most of his writings are lost, but there remain his seven books on the wars in Gaul (an eighth was added by another hand), and three

78

books on the Civil War. His composition is simple; he indulges in no images, no laboured descriptions and no conventional reflections. In dry military manner, Caesar lets the facts speak for themselves, although the facts are sometimes distorted and biased. He wrote with extreme rapidity in whatever spare time he could muster.

Caesar had gone to Gaul with four legions, but he soon found that these troops were inadequate to suppress the restive Gauls and he managed to get the Senate to allocate him four more legions. The designations of these legions were VII, VIII, IX, X, XI, XII, XIII, and XIV. Two more legions, the VIth and XVth, joined him late in 54 BC. Although the names of Caesar's commanders are known, they cannot be identified with any one legion, except that in 54 BC Quintus Tullius Cicero, brother of Marcus, arrived in Gaul and took command of the XIVth Legion.

Caesar's second-in-command was Titus Atticus Labienus, the son of a senator who had been killed in the Senate House by an angry populace. When the Civil War broke out between Caesar and Pompeius in 49 BC, Labienus was to become the only officer on Caesar's staff to desert him and go over to Pompeius. Labienus was to be killed in the final battle of the Civil War on 17 March 45 BC, on the plain of Munda. At this time, however, Labienus was Caesar's most trusted lieutenant and it was to Labienus that Caesar entrusted the army when he returned to Rome during the winter seasons.

Directly under Labienus were the generals Quintus Titurius Sabinus and Lucius Aurunculeio Cotta. They headed a staff of energetic and able officers who included Decimus Iunius Brutus, cousin of Marcus Brutus, who had already distinguished himself as commander of the Roman fleet which defeated the Veneti. Another able officer was the young Publicus Crassus, the son of Caesar's rival, M. Licinius Crassus. Another relative, Marcus Crassus, commanded a legion. Other legion commanders were Caius Fabius, Lucius Roscius and L. Munatius Plancus. In the later Gaulish campaign, Plancus distinguished himself and was eventually appointed by Caesar to take command in Gaul, a position he managed to retain after Caesar's death.

After three years of hard campaigning in Gaul, the eight legions of Caesar's army were in a high state of training and discipline. On paper each legion consisted of 6,000 men, although in reality their average strength was about 4,500 troops. Each legion had its own name and standard, a silver eagle, the emotional emblem and rallying point in battle. The legion was commanded by a legate, the equivalent of a

Right: This illustration of a scene from Roman mythology shows the arms and equipment of a cavalryman of Caesar's day. In addition to his lance he carried a slashing sword. The stirrup had not yet been developed.

lieutenant-general. The commanding officer was aided by six military tribunes, usually men of rank appointed to the legion by the Senate. Then came the 'career officers', some sixty centurions who ranged in rank and duty from a mere junior lieutenant to the *primus pilus,* who was equivalent to a full colonel. Ranks in the Roman army were closely defined, from *Cornicularius,* the officer in charge of the headquarters staff, to the *Beneficarius,* or orderly officer. The legion was divided into cohorts, each 500 men strong, with a special double-strength Number One Cohort which included the headquarters personnel.

The Roman legion was the equivalent of a heavy infantry brigade and had only 120 cavalrymen attached to it to act as despatch riders and scouts. The backbone of the legion was the *miles gregarius,* the private soldier or legionary, who also bore the slang name *caligate*-'booted one'. Perhaps a closer modern translation of this would be 'foot slogger'.

The legionary carried two long, slender throwing spears, the *pilum,* about seven feet long with a soft metal head. On impact the head usually bent and prevented the enemy from throwing it back. The range of the *pilum* was about 300 to 400 yards. After discharging these, the legionary would move in with the mainstay of his weaponry, the short sword called the *gladius,* which was 25 inches in length. A Roman army manual instructs the legionaries to 'learn to thrust rather than slash, for the Romans easily beat those who fight by slashing, and despise them. A slash cut rarely kills, however powerfully delivered, because the vitals are protected by the enemy's weapons and also by his bones. A thrust, going in two inches, however, can be mortal. You must penetrate the vitals to kill a man. Moreover, when a man is slashing the right arm and side are left bare. When thrusting, however, the body is covered and the enemy is wounded before he realizes what has happened. So this method of fighting is specially used by Romans.' The legionary also carried a semi-cylindrical shield and wore a metal helmet and breast and backplates reinforced with iron hoops.

The legionaries fought in companies, manoeuvring in sections to prearranged signals given by trumpets. These sections, companies or entire cohorts could be disengaged and the direction of attack turned as weaknesses in the enemy lines were found and exploited. Trained to fight in close units pressing constantly upon the enemy, the legionary could bring his short sword into effective play with the long curved shield offering maximum protection.

During the fighting, the legionary was protected by auxiliary troops, usually raised from subject nations, and cavalry troops. The cavalry were also non-Roman and organized in *turmae* (squadrons) and *alae* (wings) which acted as a protective screen on the flanks of the legions but were mostly used as pursuit troops after a successful battle. Cavalry troopers carried a lance some six to eight feet in length and a slashing sword called a *spatha* some 31 inches long. Auxiliary infantry carried a pike called a *hasta* which had a wooden shaft of six to eight feet in length and a metal head of 10 inches.

With each legion came a pioneer corps capable of making roads, building forts, erecting bridges, and even building ships. Among its ranks were craftsmen such as carpenters, smiths, wheelwrights, surveyors and architects. There was a medical corps, a commissariat division, the equivalent of a NAAFI for soldiers' comforts, and a provost marshal and military police corps. By 60 BC each legion also had an artillery section using *catapultae* and *ballistae,* powerful spring guns operated by twisted cords under tension, which could fire projectiles over considerable distances.

In Caesar's day the Roman army had become the most compact military force, and perhaps the most invincible one, that the world had ever seen. Ironically, the Roman army had reached its high state of discipline and efficiency out of necessity in the fight against Celtic aggression. After the Celts had been pushed back out of Italy in the fourth century BC, Rome suffered a respite before, in the second century BC, the Celtic Cimbri were pushing south again and on no less than five occasions the Roman armies were decimated by the Celts.

In 104 BC Caius Marius was elected consul and set about the reorganization of the national defence force. Until this stage Rome had been protected only by a citizen militia drawn from the landowning classes, which was raised and disbanded as and when the need arose. Marius organized a professional army with regular pay, open to all who cared to join it. The main object of his reform was to create a standing army of long-service regulars, and enlistment in the legions was normally for a period of 16 to 20 years.

Not only did Marius do away with the amateur militia–mainly Latin farmers who, when the season to plant and harvest came, would often mutiny–but he reorganized the tactics of the legions. He disbanded the phalanx method of fighting whereby the Romans charged at an enemy *en masse* and hoped their sheer weight of numbers would cause him to fly. He evolved disciplined fighting by sections. And it was Marius who gave the legions the *aquila* or eagle standard. By Caesar's day the practice of appointing amateur officers, whose claim to military leadership was their social position, had been dropped and only professionals had command of the legions.

Marius's reforms were very effective, for the new Roman army was able to face the northern invasions and finally, in 101 BC, the Cimbri were met between Milan and Turin and overwhelmed. It is reported that 120,000 were slaughtered. Rome was not to confront the grim nightmare of foreign menace for another five centuries, by which time the silver eagles of Marius's new army had spread Roman conquest to all parts of the known world.

It would appear that Caesar's plan to invade Britain had been formed as early as 57 BC when he was fighting the confederation of Celtic tribes known as the Belgae in what is now Belgium. This was the region from which a number of tribes had fled to Britain, escaping the onward march of Caesar's legions. In fact, while Caesar was in the area, many of the leaders of the Bellovaci tribe left for Britain. And he learnt that Comm, the ruler of the Gaulish Atrebates, boasted suzerainty over the British Atrebates, and that Diviciac of the Seussiones, some generations before, had ruled not only in Gaul but in Britain.

If the Greek geographer Strabo is correct in saying that the Veneti, who had initially submitted to Caesar during 57 BC, came out in insurrection at the beginning of 56 BC because they heard he was about to invade Britain and they feared the loss of the trading monopoly with the island, then Caesar's invasion plans were not only formed by the end of 57 BC but were already common knowledge.

Caesar obviously spent some time in gathering intelligence about Britain which, as we have seen, was not a successful exercise. He did, however, obtain fairly accurate geographical information as to the size of the island, its dimensions and shape. He learnt that Ireland (Hibernia) lay to the west of it and was about half its size, and he also knew where the Isle of Man was situated. He ascertained that there were other islands to the extreme north where in winter the sun scarcely rose above the horizon. When in Britain he was able to observe by measurement through water clocks that the midsummer nights in the country were shorter than those in the south of France or Italy.

Having gathered some information by the beginning of August, Caesar decided that the season was not too far advanced to try a 'reconnaissance in force'. For a usually careful general, Caesar's decision was a surprising one, in that he should undertake an ill-prepared military expedition to unknown territory so late in the season. Could it be that his political ambition overcame his natural military caution?

84

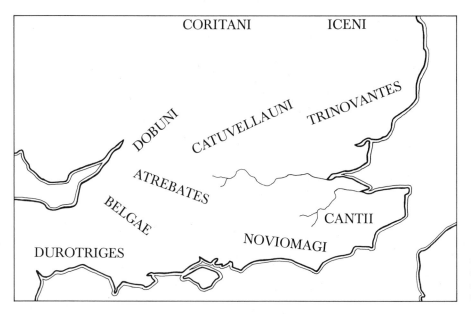

CORITANI   ICENI

DOBUNI

CATUVELLAUNI

TRINOVANTES

ATREBATES

BELGAE

CANTII

DUROTRIGES

NOVIOMAGI

Left: The tribal areas in south-eastern Britain. Caesar's main opposition would come from the Cantii and the Catuvellauni.

Caesar's preparations seemed hasty and simple. He chose two of his eight legions for his expeditionary force. These were the VIIth and the Xth. The Xth was already his favourite legion. His total force was about ten thousand men. During his absence from Gaul he placed the command of the rest of the army in the hands of his generals Sabinus and Cotta. This would indicate that his second-in-command, Titus Labienus, accompanied him to Britain, since otherwise the command would naturally have been his.

The legions were ordered to Portus Itius (Wissant) where 80 transports were assembled. These had been requisitioned from the defeated Veneti. Eighteen more transports were ordered to Ambleteuse, where some cavalry squadrons were to embark to accompany the expedition.

Traders crossing the Channel brought the British chiefs news of the Roman preparations. Gaulish refugees, who had seen the Romans in action, persuaded some of the British chiefs to send envoys to the Roman commander assuring him of their good faith. In answer, Caesar sent the chief of the Atrebates, Comm, to urge the British tribes to submit to him when he landed. At the same time he despatched Caius Volusenus in a war galley to reconnoitre the coastline for a safe landing place. Volusenus returned in five days and so, on the evening of 24 August 55 BC, the Roman invasion fleet set sail for the British coast.

CHAPTER 5

'Leap forth, soldiers!'

–STANDARD BEARER,
Xth Legion

Under the shadow of the cliffs of the South Foreland, Caius Julius Caesar summoned his staff officers and company commanders to his war galley for a general staff meeting. The task before him was how to land his force of 10,000 men on a hostile shore against a large and prepared army. The landing and securing of the beach-head was to be a purely infantry operation by the VIIth and the Xth, for he had no cavalry support. There had been a hitch in the embarkation of the cavalry squadrons in their 18 transports lying at Ambleteuse. There was some confusion among the horses and men, and the loading of the ships did not go according to the prepared timetable. As a result the fleet missed the evening tide on 24 August. Their commander finally sailed on the morning tide, but a contrary wind forced him back into harbour again. Meanwhile, Caesar vainly waited for them to rendezvous with his main invasion fleet off the South Foreland. When they failed to arrive, he decided to go ahead with the landing.

'I summoned my staff and company commanders,' he wrote, 'passed on the information obtained by Volusenus, and explained my plans. They were warned that, as tactical demands, particularly at sea, are always uncertain and subject to rapid change, they must be ready to act at a moment's notice on the briefest order from myself. The meeting then broke up.'

This 'information obtained by Volusenus' was of vital strategic importance. The previous week Caesar had detailed one of his staff officers, Caius Volusenus, to reconnoitre the British coast. Taking a fast war galley mounting 48 oarsmen, this officer made a five-day

Far left: The gently sloping beaches at Walmer against which Caesar landed his troops. The beaches were deceptively peaceful, as Caesar was to learn.

87

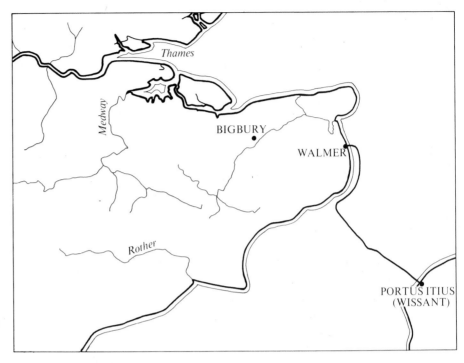

Right: The Roman fleet sailed directly across the Channel towards the coast of Britain. The South Foreland cliffs offered no suitable landing place, however, so the fleet was forced to move up the coast to Walmer.

reconnaissance along the British coastline. Along the cliffs of the South Foreland he had observed that the beach was protected by great white chalk cliffs, while further to the west an inlet gave access to hilly and wooded country. This area he did not feel was particularly suited to the landing of troops. To the east he found the open beaches of modern Walmer and Deal where a landing might be made. Had he gone further up the coast he would have discovered the ideal landing site, the great land-locked harbour of Sandwich, an area of beaches protected by the Isle of Thanet with the hill of Richborough giving a perfect site for a Roman encampment. Volusenus, however, recommended that the landing be made on the open beaches of Walmer and Deal. He reported that he had seen little else during his reconnaissance and that no hostile ships had come out from the island to challenge him.

At 3.30 p.m., having given up hopes of being reinforced by the cavalry, 'both wind and tide were favourable, the signal was given to weigh anchor, and after moving about eight miles up-channel the ships were grounded on an open and evenly shelving beach'.

On the cliff-tops the British chieftains saw the Roman fleet weigh

88

anchor and, aided by a breeze from the south, saw them work up the coast. Cingetorix, who was to be captured by the Romans in the following year, must have anticipated Caesar's intentions for, as this was his tribal area, he would have known the coastline. The British chieftains gave orders for their army to march along the cliff-tops. The massive army of mainly horse and war chariots began to move slowly, keeping pace with the Roman ships.

At the site of modern-day Walmer the British army was halted. The Roman ships were swinging shorewards. The British warriors hastened to the beaches in what, to the Roman eye at any rate, was an undisciplined and ragged formation. The Celtic battle formation was a tribal one, each tribe and each member of the tribe having an allocated and traditional place in the battle line, but to the Romans they seemed a wildly disorganized pack of barbarians.

Caesar had chosen, through ignorance, to start his landing at low tide, a time when his galleys and transports could not get close in to the shore. 'There was great difficulty,' he recorded, 'because the vessels on account of their size could not be stationed except in deep water'. The soldiers found that they had to wade over 200 yards to the shore in the face of a withering fire from the British warriors. According to Caesar: 'But the soldiers, oppressed with the great weight of their arms, ignorant of the ground, and with their hands encumbered, were obliged to jump from their ships and to engage the enemy standing close in the waves, while they on the other hand, either from dry land or having advanced a very little into the water, with all their limbs perfectly free, were boldly hurling javelins from places with which they were well acquainted, and urging on horses inured to the service. Finding my men dismayed and disorganized by this unaccustomed manner of fighting, I ordered my long-boats or galleys to be rowed a little distance from our transports, so as to attack the open flank of the enemy, and to dislodge them from their positions by slings and arrows and other missiles. This manouevre was of great service, for the British, confused by my artillery, stopped and drew back, though but for a little space.'

The artillery to which Caesar referred was mounted on the war galleys and consisted of *catapultae,* large bows fitted with skeins of hair or gut. The ends of these skeins were passed through holes bored into the frame of the box the bow was mounted on and then into large wooden washers. The skein was secured by a pin going through the centre and was tightened by hand-spikes fitted into holes in the edge of the washer and secured from springing back by catches. The bowstring was pulled

back by the winch, pulling back, in turn, the carrier in which the heavy javelins rested. Once released, the *catapultae* could hurl heavy javelins as far as 1000 yards. The range of the legionary *pilum* was between 300 and 400 yards. Even the famous English longbow of the Middle Ages only had a maximum range of 440 yards. These artillery weapons were fired from the war galleys which could get fairly close inshore, drawing four or five feet of water. They were sleek craft, 140 to 150 feet long by about 16 feet in the beam. Naturally the bulk of the British warriors had never seen such engines of warfare before and were, as Caesar says, momentarily confused. But the Roman soldiers were not quick to seize upon the lull in the battle and follow up the advantage.

'Still the soldiers hesitated to leave their ships on account of the depth

90

Far left: A Roman galley of the type Caesar would have used to transport his legions to the shores of Britain. These galleys were also engaged to cover the landing of the soldiers with the use of artillery such as the catapulta *(near left).*

of water,' wrote Caesar, 'and the temporary advantage gained might have been thrown away but for the bravery of the standard bearer of the Xth Legion who, calling upon the gods for the success of his venture, called with a loud voice, "Leap forth, soldiers, unless you wish to betray your standard to the enemy! I, at any rate, shall have performed my duty to my country and my general!" With these words he jumped from the ship and began to bear the standard of the Xth towards the enemy. Then the rest of the soldiers, encouraging one another and fearing the disgrace of the loss of a Roman Eagle, leapt down in a body from the ship; and others from the nearby ships, incited by their example, having closely followed, they approached the enemy. On both sides the battle was sharply contested. The Roman soldiers, unable to keep their ranks, or to

91

stand firmly, or to follow closely their standards, fell into great confusion, while the British, knowing the shallows, whenever they beheld from the shore any of the soldiers disembarking from their vessels, attacked them, encumbered as the soldiers were, from their chariots driven at full speed into the water, many thus surrounding a few, while others hurled javelins from the open flank on the main body of the enemy.'

As the British had been unnerved by the Roman artillery engines, now the Romans became unnerved by the British chariots. The chariot as a weapon of war was new to the Romans. Chariots were used by Romans and Greeks as a method of transport and not as a war machine. Not even the Celts of Gaul used a war chariot. Now the Romans were faced with two-wheeled and even four-wheeled chariots which carried the warriors into the attack. Tradition had it that the war chariot was introduced to Britain in the third century BC by the Parisi of Yorkshire, the tribe whose Gaulish capital still bears their name.

The chariots were elaborately adorned with decorated metalwork. The body of the chariot would seem to have been of light wickerwork with fittings of bronze and wheels with iron rims. Celtic sources speak of chariots being fitted with scythes on the hubs of the wheels which mowed down their enemies. The war chariot is featured in many of the exciting sagas of Celtic mythology. It usually contained two men, the charioteer and the warrior.

The British chariots drove down into the shallows and here the warrior would leap out and engage in hand-to-hand combat with the struggling Romans.

'On seeing this,' wrote Caesar, 'I ordered the boats belonging to the galleys and the spy-boats to be filled with soldiers and sent to help those I saw in trouble. By thus bringing into action all my reserve troops, I at length revived the drooping courage of the legions.'

At this point, according to the historian Valerius Maximus, a legionary distinguished himself: 'A certain legionary, Caesius Scaeva, having thrown himself into a boat with four men, reached a rock, whence with his comrades he threw his javelins at the enemy; but the ebb rendered the space between the rock and the land fordable. The barbarians then rushed to them in a crowd. His companions took refuge in their boat; he, firm to his post, made an heroic defence, and killed several of his enemies; at last, having his thigh pierced with an arrow, his face bruised by the blow of a stone, his helmet broken to pieces, and his shield covered with holes, he trusted himself to the mercy of the waves, and swam back towards his companions.' Scaeva was brought before Caesar. 'When he saw his general, instead of boasting of his conduct, he sought pardon for returning without his shield. It was, in fact, a disgrace

Left and above: The chariot was the most important weapon used by the British in their struggle against Caesar. The Roman coin shows a naked warrior being driven into battle, while the other objects on these two pages illustrate the attention which the Celts lavished on the metalwork of their chariots and horse harness.

93

to lose that defensive arm; but Caesar loaded him with praise and rewarded him with the grade of centurion.' The same exploit was recorded by a later Roman historian, Eutropius, rewritten from a fragment by Suetonius.

It is interesting to note, confirming that the beaches of Walmer and Deal were the sites of Caesar's landing, that the rocks mentioned by Valerius Maximus and Suetonius can still be seen at low water during the spring tides and are known as The Malms. No such rocks are to be found at any other suggested landing site.

With the commitment of his reserves, the battle for the beach-head soon swung in the Romans' favour. Caesar notes: 'The soldiers, having gained the shore and their discipline restored, made a concerted attack on the British and put them to flight. They could not, however, pursue them very far, owing to the vessels with the cavalry having been unable to gain the island through contrary winds. In this one particular my usual good fortune had failed me.' The beach-head was secured by early evening, perhaps about 7 p.m.

The Celts, however formidable in a guerrilla war, were never, now or afterwards, able to resist the Roman legions in battle formation. Rugged individualists, they were used to open warfare where they could swing their long swords against individual targets. The close assault of the legionaries in tight formation was such that there was no room to employ this method of fighting.

Sometimes the whole battle would hinge for the Celtic warriors on a hand-to-hand combat between the champions of the armies. There were strict rules about single combat in Celtic society, and Celtic mythology is full of accounts of such heroic clashes. Opposing armies would gather facing one another and first boast of their prowess; the battle would sometimes become a verbal war. Diodorus Siculus wrote: 'And when someone accepts their challenge to battle they proudly recite the deeds of valour of their ancestors and proclaim their own valorous quality, at the same time abusing and making little of their opponent and generally attempting to rob him beforehand of his fighting spirit'. The Celtic warriors had plenty of courage but little discipline to act as a cohesive army; once the battle was joined it was difficult for their leader to direct or manoeuvre them. As we have seen, the Roman officers were able, by means of trumpet signals, to disengage or move entire sections of men during the battle.

Most of the Roman and Greek writers acknowledge the reputation of bravery that the Celts had in battle, although Aristotle is somewhat

Right: A Celtic shield boss found in the Thames near London, together with an elaborate belt of the type described by Diodorus Siculus. While some Celtic warriors fought naked, others wore belted tunics.

94

grudging when he writes: 'It is not bravery to withstand fearful things through ignorance—for example, if through madness one were to withstand the onset of thunderbolts—and again, even if one understands how great the danger is, it is not bravery to withstand it through high spiritedness, as when the Celts take up arms to attack the waves; and in general the courage of the barbarians is compounded with high-spiritedness'.

High-spiritedness or not, war to the Celt was a matter of individual, hot-blooded courage, not a cold, calculated art as developed by the Romans. Nearly 2,000 years later the Celts were still fighting in the same manner; that was why the cream of the Scottish clans ran to their destruction, armed only with swords and dirks, against the withering artillery fire of the Duke of Cumberland's army at Culloden in 1745. Polybius, writing of the Celtic wars in the third century BC, sums up their attitudes in these words: 'Such was the end of the war against the Celts, a war which, if we look to the desperation and daring of the combatants, and the numbers who took part and perished in the battles, is second to no war in history, but is quite contemptible as regards the plan of campaigns, and the judgement shown in executing it, not most steps but every single step the Celts took being commended to them by the heat of passion rather than by cool calculation.'

96

Diodorus Siculus gives the Roman view of what it was like to face a Celtic army:

'Their armour includes man-sized shields decorated in individual fashion. Some of these have projecting bronze animals of fine workmanship which serve for defence as well as decoration. On their heads they wear bronze helmets which possess large projecting figures lending the appearance of enormous stature to the wearer. In some cases horns form one piece with the helmet, while in other cases it is relief figures of the fore-parts of birds or quadrupeds.

'Their trumpets are again of a peculiar barbaric kind; they blow into them and produce a harsh sound which suits the tumult of war. Some have iron breastplates of chain mail, while others fight naked, and for them the breastplate given by Nature suffices. Instead of the short sword they carry long swords held by iron or bronze chains and hanging along their right side. Some wear gold-plated or silver-plated belts round their tunics. The spears which they brandish in battle, and which they call *lanciae,* have iron heads a cubit or more in length and a little less than two palms in breadth; for their swords are as long as the javelins of other people, and their javelins have points longer than swords.'

Polybius, in recounting the Battle of Telamon in 225 BC, describes the Celtic army in these words: 'The Romans, however, were on the one hand encouraged by having caught the enemy between their two armies, but on the other they were terrified by the fine order of the Celtic army and the dreadful din–for there were innumerable horn-blowers and trumpeters and, as the whole army were shouting their war cries at the same time, there was such a tumult as if not only the soldiers but all the country round had got a voice and caught up the cry.

'Very terrifying too were the appearances and gestures of the naked warriors in front, all in the prime of life and finely built men, and all in the leading companies richly adorned with gold torques and armlets. The sight of them indeed dismayed the Romans.'

These naked warriors, of whom Diodorus Siculus says they 'so far despise death that they descended to do battle unclothed', were called *Gaesatae* by Polybius, who clearly thought that was the name of their particular tribe. However, the name simply means spearman; the word *gae,* meaning a spear, occurs in Old Irish and is easily recognizable in the Celtic languages today. They were a band of mercenary warriors, professional soldiers, paralleled by the Fenians of ancient Ireland, who make several appearances in Celtic mythology. They fought naked because of religious ritual implications.

98

Caesar records that some British warriors stained their bodies with a blue dye to give them a more terrifying appearance in battle. In the Latin designation of 'picti' or 'painted people', the Picts were erroneously thought by scholars to be a separate nationality from the Celts. Modern scholarship is more enlightened.

In the matter of fighting from chariots and as cavalry, the Romans had much to learn from the Celts. The Gaulish Celts had already become famous in Rome for their prowess as cavalry, with their tight trousers, fine physiques, flowing cloaks and legendary acrobatic skills on horseback. In future years, under the *Pax Romana,* the Roman army used Gaulish cavalry as auxiliaries, much to their advantage in battle.

The Celts took the heads of their vanquished enemies as trophies, a practice which played a profound religious role in Celtic life. The practice was described by Diodorus Siculus: 'They cut off the heads of enemies slain in battle and attached them to the necks of their horses. The blood-stained spoils they hand over to their attendants and carry off as booty, while striking up a paean and singing a song of victory; and they nail up these fruits upon their houses, just as do those who lay low wild animals in certain kinds of hunting.

'They embalm in cedar oil the heads of the most distinguished enemies, and preserve them carefully in a chest, and display them with pride to strangers, saying that for this head one of their ancestors, or his father, or the man himself refused the offer of a large sum of money. They say that some of them boast that they refused the weight of the head in gold; thus displaying what is only a barbarous kind of magnanimity, for it is not a sign of nobility to refrain from selling the proofs of one's valour.'

This custom of the taking of heads is confirmed by the deeds of the warriors in Celtic mythology. The Romans were clearly not in sympathy with the universal Celtic custom of decapitating the heads of enemies slain in battle and regarded it as barbaric. Siculus says: 'It is rather true that it is bestial to continue one's hostility against a slain fellow man'. The Celts, in turn, regarded as barbarous the Roman treatment of prisoners taken in battle, who were sold into slavery and not ransomed as hostages in accordance with the Celtic custom. A Celt might well have written: 'It is rather true that it is bestial to continue one's hostility against the survivors of a battle'.

In spite of the reckless bravery of the Celtic warriors, when the men of the VIIth and Xth Legions secured their beach-head and began to move forward in their solid phalanxes, the British lack of efficient organization and staying power as a group soon displayed itself. Against the well

Left: This relief from a Roman sarcophagus of the second or first century BC shows naked 'barbarians' in combat. Some of the British Celts painted their bodies before battle, while others wore tunics and trousers.

co-ordinated, disciplined manoeuvres of the Romans, the individualistic warriors were mown down like wheat before a scythe. Panic soon set in, and the Celtic warriors began to flee. It might have been a repeat of the Battle of Telamon. In Polybius's words: 'Some of them, in their impotent rage, rushed wildly upon the enemy and sacrificed their lives, while others, retreating step by step on the ranks of their comrades, threw them into disorder'. The Romans had won the day.

The British chieftains were well aware of what had happened across the Channel following the Roman victories – the plundering, looting of villages and taking of hostages and slaves. This initial defeat caused them to decide that discretion was the better part of valour and that negotiations with the Roman commander should be resumed. They dismissed their warriors, each man to his own farm or settlement, and, led by Comm the Atrebate, they came to Caesar's encampment.

Comm told Caesar that the British had refused to accept him as an ambassador of Rome and had imprisoned him, thus preventing him from warning the Romans that their landing would be disputed. In view

of his subsequent history, Comm could well have been lying. Two years later Comm joined Vercingetorix and the Celts of Gaul in their insurrection against Rome and, after their defeat, he was captured. Asked what his last request was he answered that 'he should never again be asked to look on a Roman face'. The request was granted for Comm managed to escape across the Rhine into Germany and eventually return to Britain as ruler of the Atrebates of Hampshire. Judging from the coinage he struck, the Atrebates emerged as a dominant political force in southern Britain. When Comm died he was succeeded by three sons: Eppillus, who ruled in north-east Kent, Tincommius in Sussex, and Verica, who ruled the main tribal lands of the Atrebates. His sons also struck many coins during their period of political dominance. Under such circumstances it could well be that Comm, who had submitted to the Roman conquest only two years previously, was still secretly anti-Roman and was not the loyal servant that Caesar imagined him to be. It may well have been that he was active in helping the British chieftains oppose the Romans.

The British, however, supported Comm in his claim that he had been imprisoned and blamed it on 'the common people', who had forced them to do it. As we have seen, the chieftainship of a Celtic tribe was an elected office and not necessarily a hereditary one, and therefore the chiefs were duty-bound to carry out the democratic wishes of the tribal assemblies. 'They asked me to excuse this unprovoked attack on the grounds of their ignorance,' wrote Caesar. Whether Comm was lying or not, Caesar accepted him back as his ambassador and chief interpreter.

As well as the chieftains of the four Cantii septs, Cinegtorix, Carnilius, Taximagulus and Segonax, there came to Caesar's encampment a young man called, by British sources, Avarwy, who was to play a prominent part in Caesar's second invasion attempt the following year. Avarwy was said to be the son of Lugh or Lud, a powerful chieftain who ruled the Trinovantes, whose tribal lands lay in Essex and southern Suffolk, and who had recently died. One source says that Avarwy was chieftain of the tribe under the suzerainty of Caswallon, whom the Romans came to know as Cassivelaunus, ruler of the Cassi (Catevellauni), whose tribal capital was at Wheathampstead, near St Albans. Caswallon's Cassi were a powerful tribe who dominated southern Britain and who seem to have migrated from Gaul, from Châlons on the Marne, and settled in Britain in the third or second century BC. The proof of Caswallon's power was that he was elected to command all the British warriors in their fight against the Romans in the following year. As it has been pointed out, later Celtic polity consisted of tribal chieftains, provincial chieftains and an overall High Chief or King. It could be interpreted from the British tribes' ready acceptance of Caswallon's leadership that he was, in fact, the High King of southern Britain at this time. Avarwy, says one source, was treated by Caswallon as his own son.

Caesar came to know Avarwy as Mandubratius, little knowing that the name he ascribed to the Briton was a stigmatic nickname, *Du bradwr* or *Mandubrad*–the Black Traitor. Avarwy was so named because his people had discovered that he had entered into secret negotiation with Caesar before his first invasion and was preparing to betray Caswallon to the Romans. Caesar says, however, that Mandubratius was the son of Imanuentius, who ruled the Trinovantes, and whom Caswallon had slain. Mandubratius, says Caesar, had asked him to restore him to the throne of his father. As the law of primogeniture did not necessarily apply in Celtic society, Avarwy probably did not have any claim to his father's chieftainship.

Peace negotiations between the British chieftains and the Roman commander went on for four days. The British made promises of submission but nothing was clarified. From the British viewpoint the talks were merely delaying tactics while they tried to reorganize their strategy against the legions.

For most of the four days the legions contented themselves with building a fortified encampment. Without cavalry, Caesar made no attempt to explore the surrounding countryside. The soldiers' provisions were brought in, albeit unwillingly, by the British from the surrounding settlements. On the fourth day, however, sails were sighted from the Roman encampment. The 18 transports bearing the Roman cavalry from Ambleteuse had finally caught up with the main invasion force. Now, perhaps, Caesar could explore the interior of the island.

By afternoon the transports were lying close inshore when a sudden squall sprang up from the north-east. The heavy ships were scattered before they could make landfall. Many of them reached Ambleteuse safely that night; others were blown down the Channel. At one point they tried to anchor, but great waves broke over them. During the night the wind died down and so, hugging the Gaulish coast, they made their way into Ambleteuse in the dawn light. It was a credit to their seamanship that not a ship was lost. For Caesar, however, it was a disaster.

The Romans not only lost the valuable reinforcement of cavalry but their own transports were smashed by the same storm. That night the moon was full and the tide almost at the springs; the rollers raced up the shingle to where the warships lay beached and filled their hulls with water. The heavier transports, dragging on their anchors, were dashed on the beach and destroyed. The Roman soldiers stood looking helplessly on. Caesar dryly recorded: 'The result was that the warships, which had been beached, became waterlogged; as for the transports riding at anchor, they were dashed one against another, and it was impossible to manoeuvre them or do anything whatever to assist. Several ships broke up, and the remainder lost their cables, anchors and rigging.'

The situation of the Roman invasion force was bleak. They were cast away on a hostile shore, a small force of hungry men with no provisions, clothing or equipment for a protracted winter campaign. There were also no facilities to repair or replace the lost transports and no reinforcements within call in case the British decided on a massive and concentrated attack. Caesar, however, was not the type of man to panic. He calmly ordered fatigue parties to go out and reap neighbouring wheat crops and confiscate supplies from the nearest villages and settlements. The year had been fairly dry and there were some good crops standing ripe for harvesting. At the same time he ordered his engineers to demolish the worst-damaged of his ships and use them to repair the others. Twelve of the vessels were found totally beyond repair. It was to be a race against time, for the Romans could feel the chill in the early autumn air and the worsening weather would make it difficult for them to chance the crossing back to Gaul.

In the meantime, the British chiefs must have considered the storm to have been sent by the gods themselves. Seeing the plight of the Roman troops, they issued orders to raise the tribes once again. This time they did not mass for an attack on the main body of the Roman forces but kept to a guerrilla warfare, ambushing isolated patrols, foraging parties and outposts. The British objective was to prevent the legions from replenishing their provisions and to starve them out with a protracted and wearying campaign of harassment.

Soon after, members of the VIIth Legion were sent to reap corn some distance from the encampment. 'Suddenly,' wrote Caesar, 'the sentries on the gates reported an unusually large cloud of dust in the direction which the legion had gone. My suspicions were confirmed – the natives had hatched a new plot.' A large force of British war-chariots was hiding in ambush in a wooded area, which archaeologists have suggested as being sited between Martin Mill and Ringwould. As the fatigue parties from the VIIth Legion marched by, they were surrounded and attacked.

Caesar issued immediate orders: 'The battalion on guard duty were detailed to go with me to the scene of the action, two others were ordered to relieve them and the rest to arm and follow on immediately. We had not been marching long before I noticed the VIIth was in difficulties: they were only just managing to hold their own with their units closely packed under heavy fire.'

Once again Caesar had a chance at seeing first-hand how the British used their war-chariots to good advantage. 'Their manner of fighting from chariots is as follows,' recorded Caesar. 'First of all they drive in all directions and hurl javelins, and so by mere terror that the teams inspire and by the noise of the wheels they generally throw the ranks of soldiers into confusion. When they have worked their way in between the troops, they leap down from the chariots and fight on foot. Meanwhile their charioteers retire gradually from the battle, and place the chariots in such a fashion that, if the warriors are hard pressed by the enemy, they may have a ready means of retreat to their own side.

'Thus they show in action the mobility of cavalry and the stability of infantry; and by daily use and practice they become so accomplished that they are ready to gallop their teams down the steepest of slopes without loss of control, to check them and turn them in a moment, to run along the pole, stand on the yoke, and then, quick as lightning, to dart back into the chariot.'

The scythed wheels of the British war-chariots created havoc among the Roman troops. The chariots must have seemed to the Romans what the first British tank was to the German infantry fighting on the Somme in 1916. Caesar's answer to the British weapon was the adaptation of the movement known as the *testudo,* or tortoise, in which his soldiers created a metal wall by linking their shields to prevent themselves from being cut to pieces by the scythes.

Caesar and his reinforcements checked his panicking legionaries. According to British tradition, the commander of the attacking force was a chieftain named Nennius who personally attacked a detachment of the Xth Legion which Caesar was commanding, and they were hard pressed to save their battle-standard from capture. The tradition had it that the sword of the Roman general buried itself in the shield of Nennius and before Caesar could extricate it the tide of the battle separated the combatants, leaving the weapon as a trophy for the British. True or not, Caesar was hard pressed to save the Romans from anything but an orderly retreat back to their fortified encampment. The Romans were unable to prevent the British from carrying off a number of prisoners and the weapons which they had captured on the field.

A period of extremely bad weather now set in. 'For many days in succession,' recalled Caesar, 'tempestuous weather prevented both armies from resuming hostilities'. During this time the British tribes had gathered for what they considered would be the decisive blow which would drive the invading Romans back into the sea. Their victory had given them confidence to change their battle tactics from harassment back to open, full-scale battle. They gathered a hastily equipped and prepared army and marched to the fortified Roman position. The Romans were prepared. The grizzled veterans of many campaigns were drawn up in full battle order, in disciplined ranks, tight lipped and silent. They were on ground of their own choosing, in fortified positions with their backs to the sea, preventing an attack from the rear, which Celtic honour would have prevented their enemies from making, even had it been open to them. They were probably backed by heavy artillery, the *catapultae,* dismantled from the ships.

Against these silent, serried ranks marched the British army, a vast concourse of warriors accompanied by a din of noise, trumpets and war-cries. Before the unmoved Roman troops they halted, taunting them, praising their own heroic prowess, daring the Romans to send out their champion for a hand-to-hand combat to decide the battle once and for all time. The Romans listened unmoved, perhaps not understanding the meaning of the shouts and taunts. But they had behind them many centuries of facing such people.

Silently they waited until the Celts, having worked themselves up into fever pitch, began their charge—a ragged, undisciplined charge, a charge such as their descendants made against the English lines at Culloden, a sudden glorious rush by which they hoped to swamp their enemies by sheer weight of numbers.

As the ragged lines of charging warriors neared the Roman positions, an order would be shouted and a trumpet's high note would resound above the din. The shields of the front ranks would move sideways and thousands of *pilumi,* the Roman javelins, would fly through the air, smashing into the Celtic charge at a range of 300 yards. The charge would falter and halt. Then, in tightly formed sections, the legionaries would march slowly but resolutely forward with their short swords.

The outcome was almost inevitable. Leaving many of their slain on the field, the British were totally routed and pursued across the countryside for a while. Caesar mentions that Comm took part in this pursuit with 30 horsemen who acted as his bodyguard and whom he had brought across from Gaul with him. Caesar closes the incident with his usual dryness: 'Envoys came to sue for peace; they were met with a demand for twice as many hostages as before, and were ordered to bring them over to the Continent, because the equinox was close at hand and the ill condition of our ships made it inadvisable to postpone the voyage until winter. Taking advantage of fair weather, we set sail a little after midnight, and the whole fleet reached the mainland in safety.'

While the British were recovering from their defeat, the Roman soldiers quietly embarked on the repaired ships under cover of darkness and set sail for Gaul. For Caius Julius Caesar it was a disappointing venture. More than once an apologetic note enters into his narrative, for all he had succeeded in doing was conducting a few inconclusive skirmishes with the southern British tribes which had cast doubt on his reputation as a soldier. Certainly the political faction in the Senate supported by Crassus and Pompeius would be quick to criticize him for undertaking an invasion of Britain, a hostile island, so late in the season. They would criticize him for not taking a sufficiently strong force with equipment, provisions and accessories for a proper campaign with the force's safety assured. They would criticize him for not ensuring the safety of his fleet in a time of uncertain weather. Overall, he could expect a reprimand for undertaking a hurriedly planned sortie, prepared with inadequate intelligence about his potential enemies.

In his defence he could maintain that his invasion was merely a military reconnaissance by which he meant to learn something of the country in preparation for a proper invasion. Already, as his war galleys pulled away from the British coast, the Roman general was planning a new invasion with at least three times as many troops and more extensive equipment–a sufficient force to conquer the whole island. A blot had been made on his military reputation and that must be erased before another year was out.

108

CHAPTER 6

'Caesar wants to murder us in Britain!'

–DUMNORIX

On his return to Gaul, Caesar sent the VIIth and Xth Legions to winter quarters in the tribal lands of the Belgae (modern Belgium) while he prepared to return to Italy for the winter. Before leaving northern Gaul he issued orders to Titus Labienus for preparations for a new invasion force. He had learnt one lesson well: a number of shallow-bottomed transports were needed to facilitate the landing of the legionaries in Britain by getting them close inshore. New transports would have to be designed.

He left with Labienus 'detailed instructions . . . for the dimensions and shape of these new vessels. To simplify loading and beaching, they were to be constructed with a somewhat lower freeboard than that commonly used in the Mediterranean, especially as I had noticed that, owing to the frequent ebb and flow of the tides, the waves in the Channel are comparatively small. To allow for heavy cargoes, including numerous pack-animals, they were to be rather wider than those used in other waters; and all were to be fitted with sails as well as oars, an arrangement which was greatly facilitated by their lower freeboard.'

Having drawn up detailed plans for the next season's campaign, which was to be devoted solely to the British conquest, Caesar set off for Italy. Some expected news was waiting for him. His appointment as governor of Gaul was due to terminate in March 54 BC, but the Senate had sanctioned a renewal of his appointment for a further five years. His rival, Crassus, had just left Rome to take up an appointment as governor of Syria, while his main antagonist and son-in-law, Pompeius, was still in

Far left: The head of Julius Caesar on a contemporary coin. This is one of the few representations of Caesar which definitely date from his lifetime.

Above: On his return to Gaul, Caesar set out to visit the various boat-building stations to check progress on the preparations for his second invasion. This illustration shows Roman soldiers loading supplies on boats during the Dacian campaign, and is from Trajan's Column in Rome.

Rome engaged in political intriguing, although he had been appointed governor of Spain. Pompeius had just opened a new theatre and was staging shows of particular barbarity which caused Cicero, returned from exile and officially pardoned, to express his disgust for the more cruel parts of the entertainment such as the ritual slaughter of 18 elephants.

On his arrival in Rome, Caesar found that he was the hero of the day. His establishment of a bridgehead across the Rhine and the invasion of Britain roused great enthusiasm in the city and the pro-Caesar faction in the Senate proposed an unprecedented period of 20 days of thanksgiving. The pro-Crassus and pro-Pompeius faction found themselves in a minority and the proposal was passed. This was mainly thanks to Caesar's political agents playing up the remoteness of Britain, the unknown hazards of the Channel and the audacity of a commander who would dare such a great military adventure.

When he visited his son-in-law, Caesar found that his daughter Julia was seriously ill with a form of shock. The elections in Rome that year had been particularly bloody, with rioting in the streets. Pompeius, addressing a meeting, had his toga stained with blood, at the sight of which Julia went into a shock from which she never recovered.

The consuls elected for 54 BC were Appius Claudius Pulcher and Lucius Domitius Ahenobarbus, whose descendent of the same name was to change it to Nero and become the most notorious of the Roman emperors. Pulcher and Ahenobarbus were men of no definite political convictions, but as it was Caesar, Crassus and Pompeius who controlled the Senate, it mattered little who held the ordinary political offices.

Early 54 BC saw the outbreak of some disturbances in Illyricum which, with Cisalpine Gaul and Transalpine Gaul, came under Caesar's control. He hastened there, but the troubles were resolved without bloodshed. By the end of April, Caesar returned to northern Gaul. With him he took two new legionary commanders. Quintus Tullius Cicero, the brother of Marcus Tullius Cicero, had been governor of Asia from 61 AD to 59 AD. More lately he had been one of Pompeius's generals commanding in Sardinia. He was to take command of the XIVth Legion and become one of Caesar's most efficient officers. His presence on Caesar's staff was perhaps a security for the good behaviour of his more politically minded brother Quintus. The tone of the letters from Marcus to Quintus at this time is one of great political despondency, and Marcus repeatedly warns Quintus to be careful what he writes. Marcus clearly foresees the rise of a dictatorship in Rome and doubtless suspects Caesar plotting to become that autocrat. The second officer to join Caesar was Caius Trebonius, the man who proposed that Crassus and Pompeius be appointed governors of Syria and Spain. Trebonius was also given command of a legion and was to remain loyal to Caesar during the Civil War. With Decimus Iunius Brutus, he was in charge of the siege of Marsilia (Marseilles). Elected consul in 45 BC, he became active in the plot to assassinate Caesar, became governor of Asia, but fell to assassins' knives in turn in 43 BC.

On his return to northern Gaul, Caesar found that his troops had worked well during the winter. There was a fleet of 600 of the new type of transports awaiting him and 28 war galleys. Caesar visited the various boat-building stations to see for himself how the work had progressed and he was hearty in his congratulations. The fleet was to be assembled at Portus Itius.

While he was making plans as to what troops he would take with him, news reached him of unrest among the Celtic tribes in the north. The Treveri, a powerful tribe on the Moselle which still refused to accept the suzerainty of Rome, were particularly restive. Caesar immediately set off with four legions and some 800 cavalry and marched into their territory. Two rival chieftains, Indutiomarus and Cingetorix were fighting for power. Caesar's policy was simple. He found out which chieftain was pro-Roman–in this case it was Cingetorix, who proved more than accommodating–and gave military aid to overcome his rival. Hostages were taken and the troubles put down within a few weeks. Caesar returned to the coast around 11 June, doubtless congratulating himself on the infallible working of the time-honoured *divide et impera* policy.

But Caesar could have been under no illusions as to the state of Gaul. He knew that at any moment the half-conquered country could erupt into violence and that his absence in Britain might well be the signal for a general uprising. He decided that any such plans might be nipped in the bud by rounding up potential Gaulish leaders as hostages and taking them to Britain. The most prominent of these anti-Roman chieftains was Dumnorix, the chief of the Aedui, a tribe which was one of the most Romanized in Gaul. For years the Aedui had been governed by Dumnorix's brother Diviciac, or Divitiacus as the Romans called him. The tribal capital was at the hill-fort of Bibracte which, about 12 BC, was to become the Romanized town of Augustodunum, the modern French town of Autun, near Dijon.

Diviciac and Dumnorix violently differed in their politics. Diviciac was a devoted adherent of Roman imperial policy and claimed friendship with Caesar. Dumnorix was a Celtic nationalist and a steadfast leader of the anti-Roman faction. It is Diviciac who remains the more complex character of the two. The Aedui had been defeated by a Germanic tribe, the Sequani, under their ruler Ariovistus, about 71 BC when the Germans began to expand across the Rhine. Diviciac had gone to Rome about 60 BC to seek Roman aid to help free his people from German suzerainty. He was even allowed to address the Senate and become known to Cicero, who described him as a druid as well as a chieftain. His appeal met with little success and, in fact, Rome formally recognized Ariovistus as a 'friend of the Roman people'.

Instead of making Diviciac a bitter anti-Roman, as his brother became, these events caused him to offer his services and those of his tribe to Caesar as mercenaries. Dumnorix, on the other hand, was determined to drive out not only the Germans but the Romans as well and establish the full independence of his people. He preached the co-operation of all

112

the tribes of Gaul to throw out the conquerors whether they were Roman or German.

When Caesar took up the governorship of Gaul, the Celtic Helvetii began to make their expansion from their tribal lands in modern-day Switzerland towards the north-east. It appears that Orgetorix, chief of the Helvetii, was also Dumnorix's father-in-law. While Caesar tried to push the Helvetii back to their tribal homelands, Dumnorix was secretly making diplomatic overtures to get the other Gaulish Celts to assist them by a campaign of harassment.

Orgetorix was finally killed and the Helvetii's military power crushed during a day-long battle which took place near the Aedui capital at Bibracte. Dumnorix was arrested and brought for trial. Diviciac, however, intervened on his brother's behalf and pleaded for clemency. The most powerful argument put to Caesar for clemency was the fact that Dumnorix was a widely known and popular figure in Gaul. In view of Diviciac's friendship with Caesar, any severe punishment of Dumnorix would hurt Diviciac's popularity among the Gauls and this would hamper Caesar in his pacification of the province. Caesar, therefore, reluctantly pardoned Dumnorix but, as he wrote later, had him closely watched.

The Romans reversed their policy of promoting Ariovistus and the Germans, realizing that their territorial ambitions would have to be curbed lest they conflict with the ambitions of Rome. The confederation of the Belgic tribes of northern Gaul had formed a tentative alliance with the Germans against the Romans, and when Caesar moved against the Germans he found himself fighting the Belgae and the Bellovaci in modern-day Belgium. In this campaign, Diviciac, now recognized as chief of the Aedui, became Caesar's ally and his Aeduian cavalry greatly contributed to the defeat of the Bellovaci.

In the meantime Dumnorix, appalled by seeing his fellow Celts fighting each other while the Romans reaped the benefit, remained unrepentant in his anti-Roman stance and unaffected by the failure of his conspiracy with Orgetorix. He seems to have had continued wealth and popularity among the Gauls and persisted in forging diplomatic connections with all the anti-Roman elements among the Celtic rulers. It is not inconceivable that Dumnorix had forged such links with the British leaders who, as we have seen, were in close contact with Gaul.

About this time Diviciac disappears from the scene; more than likely he died. Dumnorix was recognized as chief of the Aedui and Dumnorix made no attempt to hide the fact that he was Caesar's implacable enemy.

Therefore Dumnorix was among the first Gaulish chieftains whom Caesar decided to take with him to Britain rather than leave in Gaul to ferment trouble in his absence.

Under Roman military escort, and accompanied by a small band of Aedui followers, Dumnorix was brought to Portus Itius with several other Gaulish chieftains whose loyalties were similarly suspect. When told he was to be taken as a hostage to Britain, Dumnorix strongly protested and led his fellow hostages in refusing to embark. Interestingly enough, among the reasons he states for not wishing to go, Dumnorix says that he had religious responsibilities to attend to. It has been suggested that, like his brother Diviciac, Dumnorix was a druid as well as a chieftain.

When Caesar insisted and told the hostages that they would be taken on board by force if they refused to go willingly, Dumnorix told his fellow hostages that they must stand firm and do whatever should be for the advantage of Gaul. He lectured his fellow hostages on the Roman despoilation of Gaul and reminded them of their own anti-Roman stand. It was for their well-known anti-Roman actions that they were being made to pay: 'He [Caesar] wants to take over to Britain and murder every one of these people whom he dares not put to death before the eyes of their people . . . Caesar wants to murder us in Britain!' Perhaps Dumnorix's suggestion was not far-fetched; it would certainly be a convenient way for Caesar to dispose, with few questions asked, of his unwanted troublemakers.

A westerly wind which had held up embarkation dropped just about 6 July and the weather calmed excellently for the crossing. Around Portus Itius there were now concentrated eight Roman legions and their auxiliary troops and some 4,000 cavalry. Caesar had decided to take five legions and 2,000 cavalry, packing them into the 540 transports anchored in the port. The remaining 60 transports were lying weatherbound in the mouth of the Seine. In addition, Caesar had gathered some 200 privately owned vessels which, with his 28 war-galleys, comprised his total fleet. This time his invasion force numbered some 30,000 troops.

Unfortunately, we do not know the designations of all the five legions which went to Britain. Caesar mentions only the VIIth (again) but it would be more than unusual if Caesar had not taken his favourite legion, the Xth, which had already seen service in Britain. We also know that Quintus Tullius Cicero went to Britain and that he commanded the XIVth Legion, so it would be a fairly accurate surmise to add the XIVth to the invasion force. But we have no means of knowing which were the

114

other two legions, except that one was commanded by Caius Trebonius.

This time Caesar left the army in Gaul in command of Titus Atticus Labienus, who was to use the remaining three legions and 2,000 cavalry in the specific duty of protecting the harbours to which Caesar's ships might be carried on their return. Labienus was also able to see to it that Caesar's army in Britain was kept supplied with grain if their stay became protracted and supplies in Britain became unobtainable. At the same time, Labienus had to make sure that Gaul remained quiet.

The invasion force started to embark and the Gaulish hostages were told to get ready to go aboard. In the confusion of loading, Dumnorix and his Aeduians slipped away, seized some horses and rode out of Portus Itius in the direction of their tribal territory. Caesar halted all embarkation and sent a cavalry detachment after Dumnorix. Their orders were to bring the Celtic chieftain back – alive or dead.

The Roman cavalry overtook and surrounded the Aeduians and probably called on them to surrender. The Celts replied by drawing their long swords in defence of their chieftain. The Romans closed in and Dumnorix was slain, crying out, as he died, that he was a free man of a free nation.

Even the hostile eyes of Rome recognized Dumnorix to be an able Celtic leader, inflexible in his patriotism to his people and an implacable foe to their conquerors. His death was to serve as a rallying point for the Gaulish tribes who, within a few months, rose against the Romans in a vicious warfare that was to last for four years. By this same token it can be argued that, in precipitating the Gaulish insurrection, the death of Dumnorix also cut short any further plans Caesar contemplated for the future conquest of Britain.

The great invasion fleet finally sailed on the ebb tide, with a gentle south-westerly wind, shortly before sunset (about 8 p.m.) on the sixth day of the month of Quintilis, which was soon to be renamed July in Caesar's honour. (Napoleon III was wrong when he suggested that Caesar sailed on 21 July.) And with the invasion fleet sailed the young British chieftain Avarwy, or Mandubratius, as Caesar called him – the Black Traitor. Avarwy was to be Caesar's interpreter and negotiator with the British, in return for which Caesar was to place him as ruler of the Trinovantes.

At first light, about 4 a.m., on the morning of 7 July, the coast of Britain was seen receding on the port quarter; the fleet was being carried towards the North Sea. The order was issued to get out the oars and after some tiring rowing the Romans found to their relief that the tide had turned once again; they were being carried towards the coast

115

and were ten miles east of the cliffs of the South Foreland. Caesar recorded: 'The soldiers worked splendidly and by continuous rowing they enabled the heavily laden transports to keep up with the warships. The whole fleet reached Britain about noon . . .'.

The landings again took place in the vicinity of Walmer, and this time the Romans were unopposed. As the invasion fleet drew into the shore, Caesar observed: 'The enemy was nowhere to be seen. We therefore disembarked and chose a site for the camp.' It is interesting to note that traces of a fortified camp have been found near the old church in Walmer. Scouting parties were immediately sent out and some of them soon returned to the Roman camp with British prisoners. We know from Caesar that the countryside in the vicinity was thickly populated for the time and, indeed, not too far away was a British fortress whose remains have been discovered between Dover and Deal. Therefore, the Romans would probably have had no difficulty in capturing some Britons in order to find out what the state of the country was like.

The prisoners informed Caesar that 'a large native force had originally concentrated on the beaches, but had withdrawn and hidden themselves . . . when they saw the numbers of our fleet'. The suggestion that the Britons were terrified by the number of ships in the Roman fleet does not accord with the fearless character that the British exhibited during the previous year. British tradition has it that Avarwy, the villain in Celtic eyes, attended the tribal council of the Cantii chieftains and maintained that it was derogatory to the honour of the Cantii to oppose the Roman landing and kill the Romans as they struggled helplessly through the surf. He is supposed to have argued that the Celtic warriors should face the Romans as equals on a battlefield and rely for the maintenance of their liberty not on Britain's inaccessibility as an island but on the courage of her warriors. Although the argument fits in with the Celtic code of warfare, it does not seem likely that even if such advice was given the British chieftains would be foolish enough to take it. Also, Avarwy was not in Britain at this time. It is more likely that the British chieftains realized that their army was not sufficient to contest the Roman landings and therefore made a strategic withdrawal to a more fortified position.

By the evening of 7 July the 30,000 Roman troops, complete with their cavalry, had disembarked and a base camp had been established under the command of Quintus Atrius. Atrius was given ten cohorts (5,000 men) and 300 cavalry troopers with orders to protect the fleet as well as the base. The cohorts would appear to have been drawn from all

the five legions (there being nine cohorts to a legion), otherwise Caesar would have merely remarked that Atrius was left at the base camp with a legion instead of specifying 'ten cohorts'.

Above: Roman troops, led by their standard-bearers, together with the type of boats used for a seaborne invasion, as seen in a relief on Trajan's Column.

Strangely, Caesar did not issue any specific orders for the protection of his fleet. The ships were left quietly riding at anchor, the captains and pilots ignorant of the treacherous southerly winds which were blowing – the winds which were once more to prove the downfall of the invasion fleet. Caesar records: 'The army being set on shore and a proper place chosen for the camp, I learnt from prisoners in what place the forces of the enemy had camped and, having left ten cohorts and 300 horse by the sea as a guard to the vessels, I, at the third watch of the night, advanced towards the enemy, having little fear for my vessels, because I was leaving them at anchor on a smooth and open shore, and I had appointed in command Quintus Atrius.' Caesar thereby introduces a note of justification into his narrative and seeks to exonerate himself from the responsibility of the catastrophe which was to follow.

In the meantime, Caesar continues: 'After a night march of about 12 miles I came in sight of the forces of the enemy'.

117

CHAPTER 7

'They did nothing unworthy'

–CAESAR

Caesar and the main body of his army left their base-camp sometime after midnight, the third watch being from midnight until 2 a.m. It was a surprising manoeuvre on Caesar's part in that he, trusting to information given him by the British prisoners, decided on a march through hostile and unknown country during the hours of darkness. The thought that he could be leading his men into a well-planned British ambush did not apparently occur to him. However, his proverbial good luck was with him, for the Romans encountered no opposition during their night march. By first light they had covered 12 miles and were looking down the Stour valley, near Canterbury, with the sun rising behind their backs.

Before the Romans was the Great Stour river, a spot near Thanington, a mile or two west of Canterbury. Here the river was fordable but broad and deep enough to present a real obstacle if defended, while beyond it was a piece of level ground which gave ample room for the British chariots to manoeuvre. This was the site that the British chieftains had chosen for their first defensive clash with the Roman army. The Romans could see them, in the early dawn light, mustering to defend the river crossing.

Caesar writes briefly of his attack: 'They [the British] came down with cavalry and war-chariots and, by attacking from higher ground, tried to bar our passage of the river. Repulsed by our cavalry, they retired on the woods, where they had a strongly fortified position of great natural strength.'

One hundred years later, when the Roman crossing of the Medway was disputed by the British, the Roman general, Aulus Plautius, sent

Far left: The earthwork ramparts of Maiden Castle in Dorset. The fort at Bigbury near Canterbury was similar in type, although smaller; it presented few problems for the experienced Roman force.

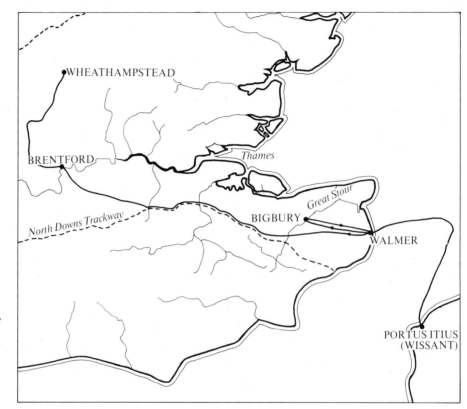

WHEATHAMPSTEAD

BRENTFORD

Thames

North Downs Trackway

BIGBURY

Great Stour

WALMER

PORTUS ITIUS
(WISSANT)

Right: After landing at Walmer, Caesar moved inland to attack the Celtic fortress at Bigbury. The destruction of the fleet forced the Romans to return temporarily to their base camp before setting out along the North Downs towards Wheathampstead, where Caswallon's headquarters lay.

across a detachment of Batavi, a Germanic tribe from Holland 'who were accustomed to swim easily in full armour across the most turbulent streams'. It would seem that Caesar sent a similar auxiliary cavalry detachment to secure the river crossing to enable his legionary troops to cross unhampered. The cavalry attack appears to have been sufficient to cause the Cantii to retire into the hills, which rose rapidly to considerable heights. In Caesar's time, the area would have been heavily wooded.

Cavalry scouts soon reported back to Caesar that most of the Britons had retired to a fortress which has since been identified with the remains of a fortified Celtic encampment at Bigbury Wood. The Britons had apparently prepared for a siege, and most of the approaches to the hill-fort had been obstructed by the felling of timber. With their main body inside the fortress, the Cantii sent out small groups to raid and harry the legionary outposts and scouting detachments.

Caesar came up and inspected the fortifications. It was a fairly simple

120

fort; the ramparts and palisades rose some 20 feet above a defensive ditch which surrounded the earthen banks on which the walls were built. He then detailed the VIIth Legion to storm it, perhaps as a chance to take revenge for their near-defeat at the hands of the Britons during the previous year.

One can imagine the Britons lining the ramparts issuing their usual taunts and jeers as the Roman cohorts marched into position, just out of bowshot and slingshot. The Britons were probably puzzled that the strange soldiers, moving in disciplined phalanxes, did not answer back with counter-boasts nor make an attempt to storm the walls in one wild rush which would succeed or fail in a matter of minutes. They must have looked on in puzzlement as a band of Roman officers rode round the fortress, the general in command of the legion looking for weaknesses. He found what he was looking for, the place along the fortifications where the wall was at its lowest.

Roman bowmen and slingmen would probably have started a fusillade at this point in order to keep the Britons' heads down while a company of legionaries marched forward to the walls, protected by their shields. Then a company from the legion's pioneer corps would move forward with shovels and, under cover of the shields held by their comrades, they would start to pile up earth against the walls. Protected by the *testudo,* against which the British missiles bounced harmlessly, the pioneers soon erected an earthen embankment against the wall of the fortress over which the legionaries could merely run up and into the fortress itself.

Soon cohort after cohort was pouring into the British fortress and it was taken with a trifling loss to the Romans. The British hill-forts never appeared to present a problem to the Roman army. Even the biggest and most complicated defensive system, Maiden Castle, fell in a relatively short space of time when, in 43 AD, the IInd Augusta Legion, commanded by the future Roman emperor Vespasian, attacked it with artillery and the *testudo* method.

The main body of Britons and the Cantii chieftains managed to escape in the confusion, but Caesar forbade any attempts at pursuit. His troops had gone two nights without rest, the first during the Channel crossing and the second during their night march, and he realized that if the Britons attacked *en masse* his troops would not be in good enough shape to repulse them. Another reason was that he did not know the country, although this had not prevented him from making his march the previous night. However, the Romans retired from the burning British fortress and set up their own encampment.

121

Bigbury, like other Celtic fortresses, consisted of an earthwork rampart atop a natural hill. Inside were huts, food storage pits, and space for the tribe's sheep and cattle. The defenders, protected by their rampart, could rain down spears and rocks on an attacking force, but the Romans had already developed the testudo technique using linked shields held overhead to assault this type of fortification.

The next day Caesar ordered cavalry detachments to overtake the fugitives, and his men had actually succeeded in making contact with their rear-guard when despatch riders ordered them to return to the camp. Caesar had received news from his base camp that dealt a severe blow to his plans.

A messenger from Quintus Atrius told Caesar that during the night of 8/9 July an easterly gale had whipped up and nearly all his vessels had dragged their anchors and fallen foul of one another. The coastline along Walmer was littered with hundreds of ships which had been driven ashore, many totally wrecked. 'The anchors and cables had parted,' recorded Caesar, 'seamen and pilots had been helpless, and heavy damage had been suffered as a result of collision'.

Caesar withdrew all his forces back to his base-camp, no doubt cursing that the same ill luck that occurred during his first expedition should dog his second one. He hastened back to Walmer and saw the wrecks himself, galleys and transports lying on the shingle beach being hammered by the full force of the rollers. An inspection showed that 40 of the vessels were totally beyond repair. The others Caesar ordered to be pulled ashore within a line of fortifications to prevent any attack by the British. These ships were to be repaired as well as possible, which meant that his troops, their morale somewhat depleted, were set to work as carpenters and shipwrights. With the men working in shifts both day and night, it took ten full days to repair the fleet. At the same time a war-galley was despatched to Portus Itius with orders to Titus Labienus to build as many new ships as he could with the forces at his disposal.

It must have been a gloomy birthday that the 48-year-old Caesar celebrated on the Kent shore on 12 July. It became even gloomier when the war-galley returned from Labienus. There was news from Rome that Caesar's 27-year-old daughter, Julia, had died. Caesar had been close to Julia, his only child. The child she had borne Pompeius – Caesar's grandchild – had also died. Now there was no common link between Caesar and his greatest rival, for Caesar's heir would also have been the heir of Pompeius. There was nothing to prevent a civil war between Caesar and Pompeius as each strove to make himself dictator of the Roman empire. Caesar wrote a letter to Marcus Cicero from Britain in which he mentions the death of Julia. In a letter to his brother, Quintus, serving with Caesar in Britain, Cicero expresses his great regard for Caesar and admiration for the firmness with which he bore his daughter's loss.

It was the second tragic blow that Caesar suffered during that year of

Right: This dramatic view of the Celtic fortification on Brent Knoll, Somerset, gives a good impression of what Caswallon's headquarters at Wheathampstead would have looked like to Caesar.

124

125

54 BC for his mother, Aurelia, to whom he was still so close, also died. The powerful influence of the two most remarkable women in Caesar's life was gone and the road to 'the Ides of March' was clearly established.

By 19 July the Roman fleet had been sufficiently repaired and Caesar was able to march his troops back into the interior, once again heading towards the Great Stour, west of Canterbury. But there had been rapid political and military changes among the British tribes. Caesar's attack and conquest of the fortress at Bigbury had been a severe blow to the chieftains of the Cantii. So far as is known by archaeological evidence, Bigbury was the most important British fortress south-east of the Thames. The Cantii had, therefore, sought military assistance.

Overall military leadership had been given to Caswallon of the Cassi. Caesar, who records his name as Cassivelaunus of the Catuvellauni, tells us that Caswallon's territory was 75 miles from the sea, north of the Thames river, and that 'until then he had been almost continually at war with the other tribes, but owing to the general alarm inspired by our arrival they had unanimously agreed to confer upon him the supreme command'. Caswallon's tribal territory stretched from Middlesex into Hertfordshire and Oxfordshire. His capital can still be traced at Wheathampstead, a little north of St Albans. As we have seen, later Celtic polity admitted of tribal chieftains, provincial chieftains and an overall High Chief or King, and it could well be that the British tribes' ready acceptance of Caswallon as 'supreme commander' was due to the fact that he was regarded as High King of Britain at this time. Unfortunately nothing is known about Caswallon except that in him Caesar met a very astute military commander.

Caesar's first march inland had met with no resistance until he reached the Great Stour. But now he felt the different personality of the new enemy commander. He had only marched a few miles from the coastline when he found his troops engaged in running battles with British cavalry and war-chariots. It became obvious that Caswallon's tactics were to harry and slow the Roman army as they marched into the interior of the island. Time and again war-chariots and cavalry would swoop down and attack the vanguard or the rear-guard, scouting parties or flanking detachments. Time and again, the Romans would halt and repulse the attacks and then resume their march. Sometimes, after repulsing the Britons, the junior Roman officers, carried away by their enthusiasm, would let their men chase the Britons into the forests. Each time that happened it spelt disaster for the Romans, for they found their units cut off by hidden British marksmen and they suffered heavy losses.

126

At the end of a difficult day's march the Roman army halted and began to prepare a fortified encampment, but Caswallon would not let the Romans rest so easily. His troops burst out of the surrounding woods and engaged the Roman units detailed to protect the fatigue parties. 'They rushed unexpectedly from the woods, attacked the outposts which were stationed in front of the camp, and some heavy fighting ensued,' recalled Caesar. He immediately ordered the first cohorts of two legions, the double-strength headquarters cohorts which contained the veteran troops of each legion, to the relief of the outposts. For a moment it seemed that these 2,000 troops would cut off the British raiders, but the British chariots and cavalry charged straight at the Roman infantry: 'The enemy, with amazing dash,' Caesar grudgingly admits, 'broke through the gap and retreated to safety'. The chariots and cavalry streamed through a gap left by the Roman troops because the legionaries were too unnerved to try to close up. Caesar records that one of his senior officers, a military tribune named Quintus Laberius Durus, was killed during this skirmish.

The British tradition, recorded centuries later, has it that the British chieftain Nennius, who led the attack on the VIIth Legion in the

Above: Roman soldiers in battle with 'barbarians'. This scene from a Roman sarcophagus depicts the turmoil of conflict once the enemy had broken through the ranks of the Roman army.

127

previous year, also commanded the Britons during this attack. But 'the success of the day was dearly purchased,' say the British annals, 'by the death of Nennius who fell in the last onset of the enemy'.

The attack gave the Romans some food for thought. Caesar recorded: 'In the whole of this kind of battle, since it was fought under the eyes of all and before the camp, it was perceived that our men, on account of the weight of their arms (inasmuch as they could neither follow those who were giving way, nor dared to depart from their standards) were little suited for an enemy of this kind; that the cavalry moreover fought with great danger, because that they [the enemy] would oftimes retreat even designedly, and when they had drawn off our horse a little way from the legions, would leap down from their chariots and fight on foot in unequal combat. But this system of cavalry engagement is wont to bring equal disaster, and of the same kind to both those retreating and those pursuing.'

He added that 'the enemy never fought in close order, but in small parties and at considerable distances, and had detachments placed about, and some, in turn, took the place of others, and the vigorous and fresh troops succeeded those who were weary'. He also concluded that although 'very many of the enemy have been killed', the Romans had 'lost some of their own, *from having pursued too eagerly*'.

He most likely held a staff meeting and gave orders that junior officers were to forbid their men from pursuing the retreating Britons.

Clearly the brilliance of the British commander, relying on these hit-and-run guerrilla tactics, can be seen. It was obvious to Caesar that Caswallon wanted to entice the Romans to pursue his men, splitting groups away from the main Roman army, cutting them off and eliminating them. In fact, the day after the attack on the Roman camp, Caesar records that Caswallon sent out small detachments of warriors who 'took up their position at a distance from the camp, on the hills, and began to show themselves in small parties, and with less spirit than on the day before, to provoke our horsemen to combat'. Caesar forbade any foolhardy answer to Caswallon's challenge, and after the Britons realized that their ploy was not going to work they retired.

Caesar was running short of supplies and he ordered Caius Trebonius, the officer who had joined his army earlier that year and who was destined to be one of his assassins, to organize some foraging parties to scour the countryside. Trebonius's troops went out. It was just what the British had been waiting for. Caswallon's army fell on the Romans as they were scattered in foraging parties across the countryside. The

British, wrote Caesar, 'flew upon the foragers suddenly from all quarters so that they did not hold off even from the standards'. The British were perhaps too confident and the Romans too well-disciplined. Under Trebonius's command, the foraging parties fought their way back to the main legionary force, obviously not without considerable loss of life. Once gathered in battle order, 'our men, making a fierce attack upon them, repulsed them; nor did they cease from pursuing them until the horse, confident of support, since they saw the legions behind them, drove the enemy headlong, and slaying a great number of them, gave them no opportunity either of rallying or halting, or of leaping down from their chariots'.

Three entire legions seem to have taken part in this first open battle with Caswallon, a battle that he had apparently wanted to avoid. Again, the British warriors had proved no match for the disciplined legions and were completely routed.

'Immediately after this retreat', wrote Caesar with obvious satisfaction, 'the [British] auxiliaries who had assembled from all sides departed nor after that time did the enemy ever engage us in very great numbers'. The auxiliaries to whom Caesar refers were probably the other tribes, the Cassi, Atrebates, Trinovantes, etc., who came to the aid of the Cantii.

The rapidity with which the British war-chariots moved across the countryside indicates once again that there were roads in Britain. Caswallon and his chariots were able to make a well-ordered retreat from the pursuing Romans, outdistancing them in their war-chariots. We have seen that, contrary to previous popular belief, the Celts *did* build roads and the extensive use of chariots in Britain seems to confirm this.

The road taken by Caswallon and probably followed by the Roman army was undoubtedly the ancient trackway which leads across north Kent from Canterbury to Rochester and then on to London.

Caswallon had not entirely departed from the scene. Having realized he could not defeat Caesar's legions in open battle, he continued to harry and slow the Roman advance by use of chariots and cavalry. At no time did Caswallon use infantry, and the British plan seems to have been to wear down the Roman troops and attempt to cut them off from their base-camp and source of supplies.

As the Roman troops marched through the countryside, they foraged and raided the numerous farming settlements they encountered and, after taking what supplies they needed, they put the settlements to the torch. Observing this, Caswallon seems to have embarked on a 'scorched earth' policy, withdrawing the people, their flocks and herds from the pathway of the advancing Roman army.

By now Caesar had learnt the identity of his assailant. Avarwy was in Caesar's camp and delegations from five southern and eastern septs had arrived with peace overtures. They obviously believed that Caswallon was now fighting a losing war and wanted to end the conflict as quickly, and on the best terms, as possible. From them it was possible that Caesar learnt that the only way to defeat Caswallon was to strike at him in his own tribal territory, which meant marching further northward and crossing the Thames. 'They told me we were not far from Cassivelaunus's (Caswallon's) stronghold, which was strategically placed among woods and marshland, and that large numbers of men and cattle were gathered there.'

The Roman army crossed the Medway near Rochester and continued on until they came to the River Thames, 'flumen Tamesin', as Caesar calls it, Romanizing the Celtic name. The word *tam* in the Brythonic Celtic languages means morsel, bit, piece, scrap, particle, whit, jot, and so on. Could the Celts who dwelt in *Lugh's dun,* the fort of Lugh, by the banks of the river, have humorously called it 'the little scrap of a river'?

Caesar mentions that Caswallon, now with a force of only 4,000 war-chariots, was already on the other side of the river. It would appear that he had crossed by a bridge, otherwise he would have surely encountered great difficulty in transporting his chariots. But if he did so then the bridge had been destroyed by him by the time Caesar arrived on the banks of the Thames.

Caesar wrote that 'the river can be forded only at one point and even there the crossing was difficult'. Two possible places for Caesar's crossing have been suggested: by Westminster, which would have been some way to the west of the Celtic settlement at *Lugh's dun,* or by Brentford. Either route is possible, but archaeological evidence favours the Brentford crossing.

Caswallon was already in position to dispute the Roman crossing. 'Large native forces appeared in battle-order on the far bank,' wrote Caesar, 'which was also defended by a line of pointed stakes; and some deserters in our custody revealed that more of these obstacles were planted underwater in the river bed.' Such stakes would have been a great impediment to the crossing and would have probably caused many fatalities among the cavalry contingents. At Brentford, part of the river is known as Coway Stakes and it has been a popular tradition that it was named after the British staking of the river bed. These stakes, according

130

to Bede, could be seen in his day (730 AD), although it seems highly dubious that the stakes Bede claims to have seen were the ones used against Caesar.

Nevertheless, the Romans seemed well able to deal with the obstacles. 'The cavalry went over first,' says Caesar, 'the infantry being ordered to follow soon afterwards; but the legionaries dashed through the river with such speed (though only their heads were above water) that they were over as soon as the mounted troops.' The Britons seem to have been unnerved by the sudden crossing. Caesar only adds, laconically, 'The Britons, overpowered by this combined attack, fled from the bank'.

A contemporary of Tacitus, one Polyaenus, has suggested that Caesar employed an elephant on this occasion which struck such terror by its novel appearance that the Britons fled in all directions. This is unsupported by any other testimony and it would seem that Polyaenus was confused by the fact that the emperor Claudius, on his visit to Britain in the wake of the invasion of 43 AD, took an elephant detachment with him.

Caesar was now in Caswallon's tribal territory. If he crossed the Thames at Brentford, as is fairly certain, his scouts, who now probably included a number of British defectors led by Avarwy, would have conducted him through the Colne Valley, past modern Denham, Rickmansworth, and Watford and so on to Wheathampstead.

If anything, Caswallon's guerrilla tactics against Caesar's advance probably intensified in their severity as the Romans neared the capital of the Cassi. In fact, Caesar admits that Caswallon's tactics were so successful that his cavalry could no longer venture out of touch with the main body of troops and the work of foraging was limited to what the legionaries could take during their march.

The Romans pressed on grimly through an apparently deserted countryside, but the woods were infested on every side by watchful enemies, waiting to seize on stragglers and scouting parties. Caswallon's Cassi seemed to be fighting alone, deserted by their neighbours. Avarwy had already convinced the neighbouring Trinovantes to seek peace terms and accept him as their new chieftain.

By the end of July or early August, the Roman troops had cut their way through the forest and marshlands and stood looking on the ramparts of the capital of the Cassi, the most powerful tribe in southern Britain.

It had been a tough march for the grizzled legionaries in which, Caesar recalled with satisfaction, 'they did nothing unworthy of them.'

CHAPTER 8

'We returned to the coast'

-CAESAR

Wheathampstead's Celtic hill-fort consisted of 100 acres enclosed by earthworks and walls. Outside was a defensive ditch which measured 100 feet in width and plunged to a depth of 30 feet. It was a formidable fortification.

Archaeologists have discovered substantial amounts of Belgic Celtic pottery at Wheathampstead, and it must be remembered that the Cassi were of Belgic Celtic stock who had arrived in Britain between the third and second centuries BC. Among this pottery was found no Roman ware. Wheathampstead appears to have been abandoned some time before 20 BC when the Cassi capital was moved to Verulamium (nearby St Albans), whose remains show Roman trading influence dating from this period. This evidence tends to support the claim of Wheathampstead to be Caswallon's capital and it would appear that, after its destruction by Caesar, the Cassi did not reinhabit it but built a new capital.

Within the Cassi capital the great herds of cattle and flocks of sheep were gathered for safety. The tribal herds were reputed to be extremely large. Caswallon prepared to defend his tribal fortress in a siege, but, using the same tactics as they had used against Bigbury Wood, the Romans stormed the hill-fort on two sides and were soon pouring over the earthwork ramparts. Caswallon, his family, and a good proportion of his troops managed to escape in the confusion but many prisoners were taken and, more importantly, Caesar had captured the livestock which was used to provision his hungry men.

Caswallon probably retired to another Cassi fortress, for there were over a score of Belgic hill-forts within the area, at places such as

Far left: The Devil's Dyke at Wheathampstead – all that remains of the great earthwork ramparts which fortified the capital of Caswallon's Cassi tribe.

133

Ravensborough, Sharpenhoe and Walbury Dells, which were built along a northern escarpment separating the Home Counties from the start of the Midlands. But the astute British leader was not finished yet. Although he had seen the Roman army march almost invincibly through the tribal lands of the Cantii, across south-eastern Britain, crossing the great rivers Stour, Medway and Thames without trouble, and reducing the Celtic fortresses and brushing aside the Celtic armies, Caswallon still refused to treat with the Roman general.

He sent a messenger to the chiefs of the four Cantii septs – Cingetorix, Carnilius, Taximagulus and Segonax – asking them to gather all the warriors they could and make a sudden attack on Caesar's base-camp. With the base-camp destroyed, Caswallon probably thought that the Roman army would hasten back to the coast and the pressure on the Cassi would be relieved. Caswallon could then reorganize his army for a new campaign.

It is a testimony to the allegiance shown by the British petty chieftains to Caswallon, and a reinforcement to the theory that he was High King, that – even in his defeated state – the Cantii chieftains obeyed his orders immediately. An army was gathered and an attack was launched on the Roman base-camp at Walmer. The camp was resolutely defended by Quintus Atrius, whose well-disciplined troops put the British to flight after some tough fighting. Many of the Britons were slain or taken prisoner. British tradition has it that Cingetorix, one of the chiefs of the Cantii, was captured, but Caesar only mentions that a chieftain named Lugotorix was captured.

It is Quintus Tullius Cicero who gives us the vital information that about this time (5 August) Caesar had returned to his base-camp, leaving his main army, presumably commanded by Trebonius, north of the Thames encamped around the Cassi capital. Whether Caesar had returned in the normal course of events, or whether he had returned because he wanted to inspect the base-camp after the attack or, indeed, whether he had returned because he had heard the attack was about to take place, we do not know. Caesar, strangely enough, omits any reference to the fact that he was at the base-camp at this time. It is only Cicero who writes of Caesar's presence in a letter to his brother Marcus.

Caesar could have been at the base-camp only a few days when, having ascertained that Quintus Atrius had things well under control, he returned north of the Thames.

The defeat of the base-camp attack was the final blow for Caswallon. 'So many losses having been received, his territories devastated, and being distressed most of all by the defection of the tribes, he [Caswallon] sent ambassadors to me to treat through Commius the Atrebatian, concerning surrender,' records Caesar. So to Caesar's camp once again comes the intriguing figure of Comm, the chief of the British Atrebates of Hampshire. Where had he been during Caesar's second invasion? Certainly not in Caesar's camp. The fact that Caesar says Caswallon used Comm indicates that he might have been in the Cassi camp and that his British Atrebates had fought with the combined southern British tribes against the Romans. Comm was certainly no unpopular pro-Roman ruler imposed by Caesar on the Atrebates. He had ruled them for over a year, taking over the tribe with Caesar's blessing after leaving the Gaulish Atrebates. But the Britons seemed happy with his rule. Even after an absence during the Gaulish uprising, Comm returned to Britain to continue his rule and to make the Atrebates one of the strongest and most influential tribes in the south. Caesar makes no comment on what he thinks of Comm but he appears to have accepted him as an intermediary with Caswallon.

The Roman general was brief: 'I demanded hostages, fixed annual tribute payable by Britain into the Roman treasury, and I strictly forbade Cassivelaunus [Caswallon] to interfere with Mandubratius [Avarwy] and the Trinovantes. After receiving these hostages, we returned to the coast.'

The actual negotiations appear to have taken some time, for Caesar and his legions did not return to their base-camp at Walmer until the end of August. With them they took the remainder of the cattle herds of the Cassi and a large number of British hostages, the first of countless Britons who, over the next five centuries, were to be sold into slavery in Rome and never see their native land again.

On reaching his base-camp once more, Caesar found that Labienus had despatched 60 newly built transports to replace those destroyed. But because of the ensuing bad weather only a small number of the expected ships managed to make the British coast. For some time, until mid-September, Caesar anxiously awaited the arrival of more transports. But the equinox was now approaching and he decided to separate his force into two, transporting the first detachment to Gaul and then ordering the ships to return for the second detachment. The reason for this was not only because Caesar had fewer ships due to the storm damage but because he had more men to transport back due to the large number of hostages he was taking to sell as slaves. It was from such sales that Caesar would finance his expedition. His second detachment embarked about

26 September. Caesar writes: 'We weighed anchor at 9 p.m. and the whole fleet reached land safely at dawn'.

It is fairly obvious that Caesar's plans for Britain did not end there. His mind was probably already turning over ideas for yet another campaign to accomplish his ambition of a conquest of the entire island and the establishment of a permanent Roman garrison. But the situation in Gaul drove all such thoughts from his mind.

The country was in turmoil. The news of the death of the Aeduian chieftain, Dumnorix, had created bitter feelings among the Celtic tribes, already resentful of the Roman conquest and occupation and suffering under the burden of paying for the Romans' needs and sending taxes and hostages to the far-away capital. In addition, the harvest of 54 BC was unusually poor. The fuel for insurrection was ready.

That autumn the spark was found in Indutiomarus, the chieftain who had suffered by Caesar's interference in the affairs of the Treveri. He became the figurehead of the uprising and three of Caesar's legions were to be decimated in the ensuing conflagration. Although Indutiomarus was to lose his life in 53 BC, the banner of Gaulish freedom was taken up

136

by Vercingetorix, a young chieftain of the Arverni, and for three more years Gaul was torn by a vicious warfare in which Caesar and the Roman army were hard pressed. As we have seen, Comm came from Britain to take a leading part in the insurrection and perhaps other British chieftains led contingents of British warriors to help their brethren drive out the Romans. The conflict banished any plans of Caesar's for further expeditions to Britain.

Gaulish resistance was finally crushed by Caesar and the Gaulish civilization eventually vanished. It was the Germanic invaders, the Franks, who gave their name to the new country which arose centuries later in Gaul. Only in Brittany – Armorica as it was then called – did the Celts survive, reinforced with migrations from Britain in the fifth century AD and taking its name 'little Britain' from the migrants. Brittany remained an independent state until the sixteenth century. It kept its own parliament until 1790 as an autonomous state within the French empire but, following the Revolution, France decided to incorporate Brittany into metropolitan France. The annexation of Brittany was accomplished after a protracted guerrilla warfare from 1793 to 1804.

By the end of the Gaulish wars, the ambitions of Caesar and Pompeius for the dictatorship of the Roman world had reached such proportions that they erupted in 49 BC into the Civil War and, although the war ended in the defeat of Pompeius, Caesar was not long to celebrate his triumph before the knives of assassins cut him down in the Senate House in 44 BC.

From the general Roman viewpoint, Caesar's invasion of Britain could hardly be described as a success. From the purely military point of view it was true that the Roman troops had gained the upper hand. Caesar had managed to resolve the question of tactics to be used against the British war-chariots, and once again demonstrated that the individualistic Celts were no match against a legion in full battle-order. On the other hand, the Celts also learnt this lesson and found they had superiority in guerrilla warfare and swift raids. Caesar, however, had come away with the impression that the southern British tribes were the most civilized in the island and with the term 'civilization' he associated 'accomplishment in military strategy'. He concluded, therefore, that the Britons of the interior would be far easier to conquer and subdue.

His descendants found to their cost that the reverse was true, and it was many years before the great northern tribe of the Brigantes was subdued. The Romans were never to conquer the tribes of Caledonia (Scotland); they had to content themselves with building a defensive wall as a

137

boundary which was named after the emperor Hadrian, stretching across northern Britain from coast to coast.

From the political point of view it could be argued that the second expedition was a success, albeit a superficial one. Caesar had placed Mandubratius, or Avarwy, in control of the Trinovantes. Also, of the tribes he had come into contact with, all had submitted before the end of the summer, including Caswallon, the 'supreme commander' of the southern British. Hostages had been taken but there was no other plunder, except cattle taken from the Cassi capital with which Caesar fed his troops. It was also true that the southern British tribes agreed to pay tribute to Rome, but the insurrection of the Gaulish tribes put an end to any such agreement and probably Comm was not the only British warrior who went to Gaul to fight the Romans there.

From the financial point of view it could be justifiably argued that it was the Britons who scored a victory over Caesar, for they managed to feed him false information about the potential wealth and natural resources of the island which, had they been known and appreciated by the Romans, might have persuaded them to an earlier attempt at conquest. Caesar was to learn nothing about the silver-bearing lead-mines, the copper-mines, the gold in western Britain (Wales) and the extent of the iron-workings and the tin-mines which, by then, had been operated for centuries. He learnt nothing of agriculture outside of the area he visited, nor did he learn of the spinning, weaving, pottery and metalworking to be found throughout the island.

After the receipt of a letter from Caesar written in Britain, Marcus Cicero wrote to his friend Atticus: 'It is now known that there is not a pennyweight of silver in the whole island, and no hope of plunder except in the form of slaves.' And, he warned his friend, the slaves from Britain would not be found to have accomplishments superior to those from other parts of the empire. Cicero reflected the overall Roman opinion which was to prevail for the next hundred years, that Britain would not prove to be a very lucrative addition to the provinces of the empire.

And so, in late September 54 BC, Caius Julius Caesar, 'who bestrode the world like a colossus', left the shores of Britain to pursue his path of destiny through the Gaulish wars, the Civil War, the defeat of his rival Pompeius, the bed of Queen Cleopatra and, finally, his end on the Ides of March in 44 BC.

In Britain his coming had left a legend, told by the Celtic bards and storytellers of the tribes. Caswallon returned to his position of dominance in British politics, having, as we have seen, moved his capital to Verulamium. He was to be succeeded by Androco, and then by Tascionvanus, who expanded the political prominence of the Cassi throughout Britain. From 10 AD until 43 AD the Cassi were ruled by a man called Cunobelinus by the Romans and whom Shakespeare was to immortalize as Cymbeline. Cunobelinus was the Latinization of the Celtic Cunobel–the Hound of Bel, Bel being one of the central Celtic gods. In proof of the growing power of the Cassi, Cunobel's new capital was called Camulodunum (modern Colchester), named as the *dun* or fort of Camulos, the patron god of the Cassi. Cunobel's capital had a defensive system which spread over 12 square miles, containing temples and a mint from which he issued coinage in gold and silver. Avarwy's Trinovantes once more paid homage to the Cassi.

It was the death of Cunobel in 43 AD that encouraged the Romans to go ahead with their plans for an invasion of Britain, for Cunobel was a ruler of such strength and wisdom that they felt only he could unite the

Left: A Roman coin struck to celebrate Caesar's victory over the Celts of Gaul. It is said that the bound figure at the bottom represents Vercingetorix.

139

tribes of Britain to dispute a Roman expeditionary force seriously. The Greek geographer Strabo, who died in 21 AD, had hitherto argued against Rome annexing Britain, in spite of the fact that he was a great admirer of the Roman Empire. Strabo argued that the trade with Britain in corn, cattle, leather and gold and other exports produced more revenue than would accrue if the island were to become a Roman province and the Roman treasury pay for a standing army and civil service to run the country. However, on Cunobel's death, Rome invaded Britain for the third and last time. It was to be a conquest that lasted for four centuries.

Cunobel's son Caradoc (known to the Romans as Caractacus) was to lead British resistance against the Roman army for nine years. He finally sought shelter with the northern Brigantes and was betrayed by their ruler Cartimandau, who was said to be his step-mother. Caradoc was a worthy successor to Caswallon. It is reported that when he was taken in chains to Rome and looked with wonder upon the great buildings of the city, he turned ironically to his captors and said: 'It is strange, indeed, that a people who have so many and such rich possessions of their own should envy me and mine. It is strange that the owners of these palaces should desire to drive us from our poor hovels.'

But this was to be in the future. When the last Roman troops embarked on the Kent beaches that autumn of 54 BC, Britain was to be left alone by Rome for 97 years. Only the tales of the bards and perhaps the decaying ramparts of the Roman base–camp at Walmer remained to bear silent testimony that Julius Caesar had set foot in Britain.

Bibliography

Although there is only one primary source for Caesar's expeditions to Britain–his own *De Bello Gallico*–the volumes consulted for background material, corroborative archaeological evidence and studies on the Celtic peoples are too numerous to give a full list. I merely give, therefore, a selected cross-section of the works consulted.

The main British traditions of the invasion, written centuries later, are found in ancient Welsh manuscripts, although much was translated by R. W. Morgan in *The British Kymry*.

The only liberty that I have taken in the quotation of sources is that I have changed Caesar's annoying habit of constantly referring to himself in the third person.

BENFIELD, Eric. The Town of Maiden Castle. Robert Hale, 1947.

CAMERON, John. Celtic Law. 1937.

CHADWICK, Nora K. The Druids. University of Wales Press, 1966.

COLLINGWOOD, R. G. & MYERS, J. N. L. Roman Britain and the English Settlements. Oxford University Press, 1939.

COTTRELL, Leonard. The Great Invasion. Evans Brothers, 1958.

CRAMPTON, Patrick. Stonehenge of the Kings. John Baker, 1967.

DILLON, Myles and CHADWICK, Nora K. The Celtic Realms. Weidenfeld & Nicolson, 1967.

FROUDE, J. A. Caesar. Longmans & Co, 1890.

FILIP, Jan. Celtic Civilization and its Heritage. Czech Publishing House, Prague, 1960.

GINNELL, Lawrence. The Brehon Laws. 1894.

HOLMES, Dr Rice. Ancient Britain and the Invasions of Julius Caesar. Clarendon Press, revised edition 1936.

HOLMES, Dr Rice. De Bello Gallico by Julius Caesar. Clarendon Press, 1914.

HUBERT, Henri. The Rise of the Celts. Kegan Paul, Trench & Trubner, 1934.

HUBERT, Henri. The Greatness and Decline of the Celts. Kegan Paul, Trench & Trubner, 1934.

JOYCE, P. W. The Story of Ancient Irish Civilization. 1907.

MACAULIFFE, M. J. Gaelic Law. 1924.

MAC CANA, Proinsias. Celtic Mythology. Paul Hamlyn, 1970.

MARKLE, J. Women of the Celts. Gordon Cremonesi, 1975.

MONTGOMERY, William E. Land Tenure in Ireland. 1889.

MOORE, R. W. The Romans in Britain: Selection of Latin Texts. Methuen, 1938.

PANTIN, W. E. P. Caesar in Britain. Macmillan & Co, 1934.

QUENNELL, Marjorie & C. H. B. Everyday Life in Roman Britain. B. T. Batsford, 1924.

RICHARDS, M. The Laws of Hywel Dda. 1954.

ROSS, Anne. Pagan Celtic Britain. Routledge, Kegan Paul, 1967.

ROSS, Anne, Everyday Life of the Pagan Celts. B. T. Batsford, 1970.

ROBINSON, Cyril E. A History of the Roman Republic. Methuen, 1932.

VINE, Francis T. Caesar in Kent. 1886.

WATSON, Albert. Cicero: Selected Letters. Clarendon Press, 1891.

Acknowledgements

MUSEUMS

Courtesy of the British Museum: pages 14 T, 14 M, 15 T, 15 B, 19, 42, 44, 45, 49 B, 52, 54, 56 BR, 64–65 T, 65 TR, 65 B, 92 TL, 92 TR, 92 CL, 92 CR, 93 TR, 93 BR, 95 T, 96, 108

Commissioners of Public Works in Ireland: page 12

Corinum Museum, Cirencester: pages 33, 91–Ermin St Guard

Gloucester City Museum: page 56 BL

Liberia Antiquaria Moretti: page 117

Musée des Antiquités Nationales: page 31

Musée Borély, Marseille: pages 100, 101

Musée Louvre: page 77

Musée St Germain-en-Laye: pages 35, 68–69

National Museum of Antiquities, Scotland: page 48 T

National Museum, Copenhagen: pages 47, 50, 51

National Museum of Ireland, Dublin,: pages 37, 38 L, 38 TR, 48 B, 55, 95 B

National Museum, Prague: page 24

Württembergische Landesmuseum, Stuttgart: page 49 T

Vatican Museum: Jacket

PICTURE AGENCIES

Aerofilms Ltd: pages 6–7

Alinari: pages 72, 80–81, 90

Angelo Hornak Library: pages 8, 86, 118

Photo Belzeaux-Zodiaque: pages 24, 50, 51, 68–69, 100

Janet Bord: pages 57, 61, 132

C M Dixon: titlepage, pages 45, 110

Photographie Giraudon: page 77

IGDA: pages 18 T, 98, 117, 140

Photoresources: pages 22, 33, 47, 59, 127, 136

Photo Jean Roubier: page 101

West Air Photography: page 125

PUBLISHERS

Hamlyn: Endpapers, pages 12, 37, 38 L, 48 B, 49 T, 64–65 T, 68–69

Weidenfeld and Nicolson: pages 19, 42, 44, 48 T, 56 BL, 56 BR, 65 TR, 65 B, 72, 80–81, 90, 93 TL, 108

Index